WIMBLEDON'S SERMON

Redde Rationem Villicationis Tue:

A Middle English Sermon of the Fourteenth Century

Duquesne Studies, Philological Series
9

WIMBLEDON'S SERMON

REDDE RATIONEM VILLICATIONIS TUE:

A Middle English Sermon of the Fourteenth Century

Edited by

IONE KEMP KNIGHT
Associate Professor of English
Meredith College

DUQUESNE UNIVERSITY PRESS
Pittsburgh, Pa.
Editions E. Nauwelaerts, Louvain

DUQUESNE STUDIES

PHILOLOGICAL SERIES

PREFACE

A critical edition of Wimbledon's sermon, "Redde rationem villicationis tue," was first suggested in 1951 for a dissertation at the University of North Carolina by Professor Arnold Williams of Michigan State College; the dissertation was read and criticized by Professors Norman E. Eliason and William S. Wells. However, it is to Professor Robert A. Pratt, now at the University of Pennsylvania, that I am most indebted for his scholarly guidance throughout my work on the dissertation and for his later help concerning publication. I owe special thanks to Professor Mary Lynch Johnson of Meredith College for her encouragement, valuable criticism, and advice concerning linguistic details.

I wish to thank the Reference Librarians of the University of North Carolina and Miss Hazel Baity of the Meredith College Library for their help. Mr. A. R. B. Fuller, Librarian of St. Paul's Cathedral was most gracious in his efforts to locate early prints in his library; Lord Tollemache allowed me to examine one of his manuscripts at Helmingham Hall, as did the Librarians at the British Museum; Corpus Christi College, Cambridge; Gonville and Caius, Cambridge; Magdalene College, Cambridge; Trinity College, Cambridge; University College, Cambridge; and the Bodleian Library, Oxford.

To the group of librarians and to the librarian at the Huntington Library, I am also grateful for their kindness in allowing me to have microfilms made of manuscripts in their libraries.

The Master and Fellows of Corpus Christi College, Cambridge, have kindly given their permission to print the text of Corpus Christi MS. 357.

TABLE OF CONTENTS

Chapter I

PRELIMINARY REMARKS

The Middle English sermon, *"Redde rationem villicationis tue,"* evidently preached about 1388 by Thomas Wimbledon at Paul's Cross, London, is extant in thirteen English[1] and two Latin manuscripts of the fourteenth and fifteenth centuries. There are eighteen printed editions in the sixteenth and seventeenth centuries, the first being in 1550; the sermon also appears in Foxe's *Acts and Monuments* (1562) and in an eighteenth century collection, *Phoenix Britannicus* (1731).

More recently, in 1925, K. F. Sundén, in *Göteborgs Högskolas Årskrift*, edited the text of one of the English manuscripts, Hatton MS. 57.[2] Miss Dorothy Everett, in her review of Sundén's edition, makes note of the obvious errors in the Hatton manuscript; "the collation of MS. Hatton 57 with the other manuscripts," she says, "would have added to the value of the book."[3]

There is little scholarship dealing with the sermon. G. R. Owst, in *Preaching in Medieval England* and in *Literature and Pulpit in Medieval England*, relates this sermon, along with other medieval sermons, to the intellectual milieu of its time. He says of it: "There can be no single sermon by an Englishman of our two centuries [14th and 15th] of which so many copies in contemporary manuscript, and later printed book, can be found than one of the favourite text: 'Redde rationem villicationis tuae.' "[4] Maclure calls it "the most famous sermon ever delivered at Paul's Cross."[5]

The establishment of the text itself, based on examination of the thirteen English manuscripts, has been the primary objective of this edition. The text is a critical one based on Corpus Christi MS. 357, the

[1]One English manuscript belonging to John Edwin Wells has been lost. See "Chapter II: Descriptions of the Manuscripts and Prints," p. 3. footnote 1.

[2]K. F. Sundén, editor, "A Famous Middle English Sermon (MS. Hatton 57, Bodleian Library) Preached at St. Paul's Cross, London, on Quinquagesima Sunday, 1388," *Göteborgs Högskolas Årskrift*, XXXI (1925), xv + 36.

[3]Dorothy Everett, Review of Sundén's edition, *Year's Work in English Studies*, VI (1925), 102.

[4]G. W. Owst, *Preaching in Medieval England* (Cambridge, 1926), p. 360.

[5]Millar Maclure, *The Paul's Cross Sermons, 1534-1642* (Toronto, 1958), p. 144.

manuscript which collation proves to be closest to the reconstructed common original; the important variants of all the English manuscripts are listed at the bottom of each page.

I have corrected the Corpus Christi text in certain readings where it is distinctly inferior to the reconstructed common original. These corrections are grouped together in the critical apparatus; by combining these variants with the text, the reader will obtain a diplomatic text of Corpus Christi MS. 357.

Along with the text, my study includes a description of the manuscripts and prints; an investigation of the relationship of the manuscripts; an analysis of the sermon which includes information concerning the date, author, and place of delivery; and a study of the language of the basic text, Corpus Christi MS. 357. Analogues or sources of passages in the sermon are found in the notes following the text; the glossary contains distinctive Middle English words.

Chapter II

DESCRIPTIONS OF THE MANUSCRIPTS AND PRINTS

A. THE MANUSCRIPTS

There are fifteen extant manuscripts of "Redde rationem villcationis tue," thirteen English and two Latin.[1] A list of the manuscripts and the symbols used in this edition follows:

English:
   C—Cambridge, Corpus Christi 357
   A—British Museum, Additional 37677
   H2—Helmingham Hall LJ II 2 (Helmingham Hall, Stowmarket, Suffolk)
   H9—Helmingham Hall LJ II 9 (in British Museum)
   Hr—British Museum, Harley 2398
   Ht—Oxford, Bodleian, Hatton 57
   Hu—Huntington Library HM 502
   P—Cambridge, Magdalene College, Pepys 2125
   Ra—British Museum, Royal 18 A xvii
   Rb—British Museum, Royal 18 B xxiii

[1]John Edwin Wells, *A Manual of the Writings in Middle English 1050-1400* (New Haven, 1916). Supplements I-VIII (1918-1941). Supplement IX by Beatrice D. Brown, Eleanor K. Heningham, and Francis Lee Utley (1945).

In the Second Supplement to the *Manual* (p. 1057), Wells states that he himself owned a manuscript of the sermon and that an edition of it was in preparation. There is no trace of the manuscript or of the edition. Professor Robert A. Pratt kindly made numerous inquiries concerning the whereabouts of this Wells manuscript. In reply (July 26, 1951), Professor Albert C. Baugh wrote Mr. Pratt that he knew that Wells had owned the *Redde rationem* manuscript, but he knew no more concerning it. The most definite information came from Professor Dorothy Bethurum: she wrote (August 22, 1951) that if the Wells Manuscript existed "it is almost certainly irrecoverable now . . . His [Wells'] will stipulated that *all* his papers, mss., etc. were to be destroyed." In her own examination of Wells' papers, Miss Bethurum found "no medieval mss., in fact, no mediaeval texts or material of any kind." The Wells Manuscript, apparently lost, is the only manuscript of the sermon which has not been examined.

S—Cambridge, Sidney Sussex 74
T—Cambridge, Trinity 322
U—Oxford, University College 97

Latin:
G—Cambridge, Gonville and Caius 334
Ul—Cambridge, University Library Ii III 8

Descriptions of the individual manuscripts follow.

1. ENGLISH MANUSCRIPTS

C—*Cambridge, Corpus Christi MS. 357*

Library of Corpus Christi College, Cambridge University, Cambridge, England. See Montague Rhodes James, *A Descriptive Catalogue of the Manuscripts in the Library of Corpus Christi College Cambridge* (2 v., Cambridge, 1912), II, 190-191. Wells, *Manual*, Fourth Supplement, p. 1286.

Paper and vellum, measuring $10\frac{7}{10}$ x $7\frac{3}{5}$ inches; divided into two sections: I. ff. 2 + 261, fifteenth and early sixteenth centuries; II. ff. 1 + 13, fourteenth century.

Contents:

    I. In quires of 8: 250 ff. written.
        Interpretatio skeltoni poetae Laureati.
        Most reverent holy fader ther ne hath be wryter of maters in tyme of seasons passid. ············
           —lete diodorus hymself haue the langage.
        Thus endeth the prohemye of Poggius.
        Diodori siculi historiarum Priscarum a Poggio ref.
        The Prohemy of Diodorus thauctoru:
           Men ar hyghly bounde of a congruence.
           Ends imperfectly in lib. v, f. 249[b]:
           The peple shold bee rewlyd and gouernyd to the prosperous wele in comyn.
        ff. 251-261 blank.
    II. A quire of 14. Vellum, double columns of 34 lines.
        Redde racionem villicationis tue Luce sexto decimo.

Ownership: On folio is written: "Iste liber constat Robar Peid (or pew)." Nothing more is known concerning the private ownership of the manuscript.

Wimbledon's Sermon: "Redde racionem . . ." is the only selection found in the second division of the manuscript. The text is complete and has been chosen as the basic manuscript of this edition.[2]

The pages are written in double columns with 34 lines in each column. Pagination is in a late hand. The first folio has been blotted, possibly by

[2] See "Chapter VI: The Text and Editorial Principles," p. 55.

water. In the middle of each folio is a fold, which is approximately one-half inch wide at the outer edge and in three inches gradually decreases to nothing; with care the vellum can be straightened. Tiny holes in folio 1 efface a few scattered letters; however the continuity of the text is not broken by a larger hole in folio 9.

There are no illuminated capitals; a blank space with a small letter notation for the illuminator has been left. There are capitals which were not to be illuminated; in most cases these follow paragraph marks. Most paragraph marks are by a later hand in red ink. Phrases are sometimes separated by an inverted semicolon or by a light vertical line. Some few words have been inserted by the same hand either above the line of the text or in the margin.

Common abbreviations are frequently found for *and, er, ra, ur, m, n, . . . is.* Marginalia and textual insertions are in the same hand as the text.

The hand of the sermon is a rather rough, clear one. S. H. Thompson of the Department of History, University of Colorado, analyzes the hand as chartist; the scribe, he thinks, was trained at court about 1360-1365; he states that the *er, ra* abbreviations indicate that the scribal training was in Latin.

A—B. M. Additional MS. 37677

British Museum. See *Catalogue of Additions to the Manuscripts in the British Museum in the Years 1906-1910* (London, 1912), pp. 102-103; Wells, *Manual,* Fourth Supplement, p. 1266.

Vellum; 9 x 6 inches; ii + 107 folios; early fifteenth century.
Contents:

Theological Tracts in *Latin* and *English*, viz.:
   1. 'Summa Qui bene presunt': the treatise by Richard de Wethershed, al. Grant, al. de Leicester, Archbishop of Canterbury (1229-1231), preceded by a table of chapters.   f. 4
   2. 'This sermoun was seid of a worþi clerk maistir Richard Alkartoun at Seint Marie spitel in Eestir woke þe ʒeer of our Lorde. a þousand four hondred and sixe.'   f. 57
   3. Translation of part of the Somme Le Roi of Frerè Laurent, Confessor to Philip III of France.   f. 61[b]
   4. 'Redde racionem villicacionis tue': sermon on Luke xvi. 2.   f. 84
   5. 'Sermo secundus,' an anonymous sermon on John vi. 5.   f. 98[b]
   6. Sermon, attributed elsewhere to John Wycliffe . . . beg. 'Our lorde Jesu Crist techeþ vs to praie euermore for alle nedful þyngis.'   f. 101

Ownership: Before the acquisition by the British Museum in 1908, this manuscript belonged to the library of the Archdeaconry of Huntington.

Wimbledon's Sermon: The text of the sermon is complete. Each page contains 37 lines. There is a hole in the middle of folio 96; the text is written continuously on each side of the hole.

The sermon is in a hand different from that of the preceding treatise. The beginning capital is illuminated. Other capitals are not illuminated, and are usually found after the paragraph marks. The paragraph marks are delineated in red and blue ink.

The scribe has frequently used the common abbreviations for *and, ur, er, ra, m, n.* The majority of the marginal references are in the same hand as the text, although a few references are in a later hand. Occasionally the original scribe has inserted words of the text above the line, as if added later.

There is no incipit or explicit.

H2—Helmingham Hall MS. LJ II 2

Library of Lord Tollemache, Helmingham Hall, Stowmarket, Suffolk. See *Historical Manuscripts Commission Report I* (London, 1870), p. 61; Wells, *Manual*, Sixth Supplement, p. 1449. Carlton Brown, *A Register of Middle English Religious and Didactic Verse* (2 v., Oxford, 1916) I, 471; II, 236.

Vellum; octavo; dated as around 1400.

Contents:

> Sermones moralissimi atque ad populum utilissimi supra evangelia dominicarum totius anni, a venerabili magistro Johanne Quintino noviter visi et adunati, incipiunt feliciter.
> Redde rationem villicationis tue.

Wimbledon's Sermon: The text of the sermon is incomplete because of missing and torn pages, apparently lost before the manuscript was bound in its present binding. The first part of the sermon is intact, but only the beginning and end of the second part remain. The following lines are missing: 668-774; 788-814; 828-986. A hole in one page of the manuscript obliterates a few words of the text.

The pages of the manuscript are not numbered. The sermon is in the same hand as the John Quintin sermons which precede "Redde rationem." The beginning capital and a few paragraph marks are in red ink.

The marginal references are in the same hand as the text. On the first few pages a later hand has inserted a few words above the line and in the margin. Occasionally *þ* is spelled out *th;* there are few abbreviations.

There is no incipit, but a later hand adds at the end of the manuscript: "Explicit tractatus cujusdam patris minoris qui vocabatur frater Nicolaus de atque villa."

H9—Helmingham Hall MS. LJ II 9

British Museum. See *Historical Manuscripts Commission, Report I* (London, 1870), p. 61; Wells, *Manual*, Sixth Supplement, p. 1449; Brown, *Register*, I, 471; II, 236.

Parchment; duodecimo; 48 folios; dated 1400.
Contents:

'Of Maumetrie'.	f. 1ʳ
'Which ben trewe myraclis and which ben false'.	f. 8ᵛ
'Howe men shulden gon on pilgrymage but not in maner that men usen nowadaies'.	f. 12ᵛ
'A short rule of lif for ech man in general and for prestis and lordis and laboreris in special and hou ech man shal be saued in his deye'.	f. 14ᵛ
'Redde rationem villicationis tue'.	f. 17ʳ
'There ben eiʒte conditions of mawmetrie þat men vsen aboute ymages'.	f. 37ʳ
'Be ʒe sugetis to al creature of men for goddis sake'.	f. 42ᵛ

Ownership: The manuscript belonged to the late Lord Tollemache. Along with other valuable manuscripts it was taken, at the beginning of World War II, from Helmingham Hall, Stowmarket, Suffolk, and deposited in the British Museum.

Wimbledon's Sermon: The manuscript is well preserved. There are 30 lines of the text on a page. The edge of folio 30 is torn, and a marginal reference thus lost.

The entire manuscript is in the same hand. There are no illuminated capitals; there is only the blank space in the manuscript with a small letter notation for the illuminator. Occasional words and phrases have been underlined in red ink; paragraph marks are also in red; these are usually followed by small non-illuminated capitals.

The usual abbreviations are found. The majority of the marginal notations are in the same hand as the text; the scribe has supplied in the lower margin of folio 29ᵛ four lines which he had omitted; other words throughout the manuscript he has inserted above the line. A later hand can be detected in a few of the marginal notations; on folios 30ᵛ and 31ʳ a later writer has copied a section from an Augustinian letter, the source for a passage of the text found on folio 30ᵛ.

The incipit, written in red by the original scribe, reads: "This sermon followynge was seid at Poulis in London þe ʒeer of our lord 1389." Following the last *Amen* he writes: "It endiþ."

Hr—B. M. Harley MS. 2398

British Museum. See *Catalogue of the Harleian Manuscripts in the British Museum* (4 v., London, 1801), II, 684-686; Wells, *Manual*, Fourth Supplement, p. 1266.

Parchment; octavo; no date given in the catalogue.

Contents:

Ownership: Robert Harley, first Earl of Oxford, began the collection of manuscripts, of which this is one, in the eighteenth century. In 1753 the collection was sold to the British nation by the wife of Edward, second Earl of Oxford, son of Robert Harley.[3] The manuscript is now in the British Museum.

Wimbledon's Sermon: This manuscript, like *P* and *T*, the other two manuscripts in Group *b*,[4] has a section missing in the second part of the sermon, lines 764-1026.

The beginning *R* of *Redde* is illuminated in blue and red. Also in blue and red are the paragraph marks, for which space has been left in the text. Proper names and words which follow the paragraph marks are usually capitalized. The punctuation consists of periods and vertical lines. There are 31 lines on a page.

Abbreviations are used less frequently in the Harley manuscript than in many of the other manuscripts of the sermon. Marginal references are found both in the hand of the text and in a later hand. The same later hand has supplied certain phrases or sentences omitted by the first

[3] *Dictionary of National Biography*, ed. Sir Leslie Stephen and Sir Sidney Lee (22 v., Oxford, 1949-1950), III, 1280.

[4] See "Chapter III: Relationship of Manuscripts. A. English Manuscripts," p. 27.

scribe, or has corrected readings of the text. For example, on folio 144ʳ *seculeres* has been canceled, and *rybaudys or cheerlys* written in the margin. Another time the scribe has translated a Latin phrase; on folio 141ᵛ the text reads: "Redde rationem villicationis tue," and the later hand has translated in the lower margin: "ʒelde rekenynge of þy baily."

The incipit is written in the same hand as the sermon, and reads: "Sermo Magistri Thome Wymyldone, apud Crucem in cimiterio Sancto Pauli London."

Ht—Oxford, Bodleian, Hatton MS. 57

Bodleian Library, Oxford. See Falconer Madan, H. H. E. Craster, and N. Denholm-Young, *A Summary Catalogue of Western Manuscripts in the Bodleian Library at Oxford*, (6 v., Oxford, 1937), II, pt. 2, pp. 801, 822; Wells, *Manual*, Fourth Supplement, p. 1266; K. F. Sundén, editor, "A Famous Middle English Sermon (MS. Hatton 57, Bodleian Library) Preached at St. Paul's Cross, London, on Quinquagesima Sunday, 1388," *Göteborgs Högskolas Årskrift*, XXXI (1925), xv + 36.

Parchment; 8 x 5⅝ inches; ii + 38 pages; dated by the catalogue as about 1400, though Sundén (*op. cit.*, p. v) contends that the linguistic evidence within the sermon points to a date later than 1400.

Contents:

Redde rationem villicationis tue.	pp. 1-32
two leaves from a Latin noted breviary (not Sarum or York or Hereford).	pp. 33-36

Ownership: The collector of the Hatton manuscripts was the eldest son of the Elizabethan Sir Christopher Hatton. From his library Robert Scott purchased the collection and in turn sold it to the Bodleian Library in September, 1671.

Wimbledon's Sermon: The text itself is complete except for scattered phrases or sentences which have been carelessly omitted by the scribe. Either 30 or 31 lines are found on a page. The pagination was done by a quite late hand. In places the text is blurred by blotches or smears. The corner of the folio of pages 23-24 is torn, but no part of the text is lost.

There are no illuminated capitals. For punctuation a light, vertical stroke is occasionally found; other punctuation, consisting of commas, colons, or periods, has been supplied by a later hand. At frequent intervals a late hand has placed in the margin or in the text a type of paragraph mark. Attention has been directed to certain passages by underlining and by special marks, both in a late hand.

The usual abbreviations are found. The majority of the marginalia are in a late hand. Occasionally the late hand has written glosses over words whose meaning had become obscure. For example on page 31 the reading *meynye* has been glossed *compani*. On page 5 a sentence reads: "if þou canst I rede þat þou tari not for to lerne"; a late hand has written in the lower margin: "if thou cannot I counsel thee without delay to learn."

"Wimbledons Sermon, Camden" has been written by a late hand in the upper margin of page 1; along with this notation is the manuscript number and the Bodleian stamp.

Hu—*Huntington Library, MS. HM 502*

Henry E. Huntington Library, San Marino, California. See Seymour de Ricci and W. J. Wilson, *Census of Medieval and Renaissance Manuscripts in the United States and Canada* (3 v., New York, 1935-1940), I, 71; Wells, *Manual*, Seventh Supplement, p. 1571.

Vellum; 14 x 10 cm.; 90 folios; early fifteenth century.

Ownership: The manuscript was owned c. 1500 by John Baker and later in the sixteenth century by John Wood. Around 1780 it was given by Richardson of Leeds to Dr. Richard Breene's museum at Lichfield, but was later sold to Walter Honeywood Yates of Bromsberrow Place. Sir T. Phillipps obtained the manuscript about 1845, and finally in 1925 the Huntington Library acquired the volume.

Contents:

Devotional treatises in English prose:
Robert Wimbledon, Sermon on Luke xvi. 2.	ff. 1^r-26^v
Richard Rolle, Form of perfect living.	ff. 27^r-34^r
Draft of a letter from a student to his parents.	f. 34^v
Dialogue of a priest and a nun.	ff. 35^r-60^v
S. Edmund (Rich) of Poyunteney, The myrour of holy chirche, sermon.	ff. 60^v-74^r
Various prayers.	ff. 74^v-90^r

Wimbledon's Sermon: Several folios must have been taken from the manuscript after it was assembled, for the end of Wimbledon's sermon and the beginning of the following treatise are not there; from Wimbledon's sermon the following lines are missing: 117-153; 302-339; 1042-1102. There are 22 lines on a page. Only the first page is numbered, and this number is in a late hand.

The beginning capital of each of the two parts of the sermon is illuminated; no other capitals are found. Punctuation, consisting of periods or reversed semicolons, is rare. The paragraph marks and the incipits of the two parts are written in a different ink.

Abbreviations are relatively few. Words and phrases have been inserted both by the hand that wrote the sermon and by a later hand. The erasure of an occasional word has left a blank space in the manuscript; in other places an incorrect reading has been cancelled. A few glosses in a later hand are seen; for example, *vnmyȝty* is glossed in the margin as *not able*. There are only four marginal references, and these are in the same hand as the sermon.

Pepys MS. 2125

Pepys Library, Magdalene College, Cambridge. See *Bibliotheca Pepysiana: Pt. III. Medieval Manuscripts*, compiled by M. R. James (London, 1923), pp. 72-79; Wells, *Manual*, Sixth Supplement, p. 1449; Brown, *Register*, I, 219; II, 236.

Vellum and paper; $11\frac{3}{10}$ x $7\frac{9}{10}$ inches; ff. 2 + 145 + 1; fifteenth century.

Contents:

Ownership: The manuscript, acquired by Samuel Pepys (1632-1703), was bequeathed with the remainder of his library to the Master and Fellows of Magdalene College, Cambridge. It was transferred to the college in 1724, and in 1854 to the new Masters Lodge, where the Biblioteca Pepysiana is now found.

Wimbledon's Sermon: Like *Hr* and *T*, the other two manuscripts in Group *b*,[5] the text of the Second Part of the sermon is incomplete, lines 764-1026 being missing.

Each page contains from 36 to 38 lines. The pagination is dim and often unreadable; the pages are in good condition except for f. 73, the margin of which is torn.

The sermon is in a clear hand. The capitals are not illuminated; paragraph marks in different color ink are scattered throughout the text. Punctuation consists of colons and inverted semicolons; often significant words and sources, which are included in the text rather than being placed in the margin, are underlined in a different ink.

There are few abbreviations. A few mistakes in copying are crossed out and followed by the correct reading.

The incipit in a late hand reads:

R. Wimbledon his Sermon at Pauls Crosse, 1388, in the Raigne of Henry the 4, on Luke 16, v. 2.
Printed by John Charleward 1588 in 8ᵛᵒ (and divers times since).

The explicit in the same hand as the sermon reads:

Sermo Thome Wymbeldone, London predicatur ad crucem in cimiterio ecclesiae Sancti Pauli.

Ra—B. M. Royal MS. 18 A xvii

British Museum. See George F. Warner and Julius P. Gilson, *Catalogue of Western Manuscripts in the Old Royal and King's Collections* (4 v., London, 1921), II, 268-269; Wells, *Manual*, Fourth Supplement, p. 1266.

Vellum; 10 x 7 inches; 199 folios; fifteenth century.

Contents:

See "Chapter III: Relationship of Manuscripts. A. English Manuscripts," p. 27.

Sermons in English:
  1. Homilies on the gospels for Sundays throughout the year.   f. 1
  2. Sermon on Luke xvi. 2. Redde rationem.   f. 184ᵇ

Ownership:

The manuscript once belonged to Edward Jones, " 'Predicator et rector de Tradog'(?)" (f. 127ᵇ). "Ed. Jones owith this booke" is written on several folios (see f. 185ᵇ). In his hand are Welsh inscriptions:

  " 'Resgob Morgan yw fy meistr i ne a fydd kyn duw pasc drwy ganiat duw tad,' i.e. 'Bishop Morgan is my master or will be before Easter day by permission of God the Father' (fol. 169ᵇ), perhaps referring to Henry Morgan, elected Bishop of St. Davids 26 Mar. 1554."
  'Kariad Edward Jones yw Kariad Katherin Wynne o Foeliwrch (?) ai wraig ar fyrder y duw yn y blaen' (fol. 170ᵇ).

On the last folio has been erased a fifteenth or sixteenth century inscription of a London rector, and another hand has written:

  'He þat stelys this booke, shul be hanged on a crooke.
  He that this booke steele wode, sone be his herte colde.
  That it mow so be, seiþ amen, for cherite.
  Qui scripsit carmen, Pookefart est sibi nomen,
  Miller jingatur (*sic*), qui scripsit sic nominatur.'

This manuscript was one of the 336 belonging to John Theyer of Cooper's Hill, Brockworth, Bloucester. His grandson, Charles Theyer, sold the collection to Robert Scott, from whom Charles II purchased it for the Royal library, where it remained until the Act of 1753, which incorporated the Royal Library in the British Museum. (Warner and Gilson, I, xxxi; II, 396)

Wimbledon's Sermon: There are no folios missing from the manuscript of Wimbledon's Sermon. There are 26 lines on a page. The vellum is not in the best of condition; there are holes in folios 189 and 191, but the continuity of the text is not impaired. Tears in the vellum of folios 193, 195, and 198 have been sewn. The pagination has been done by a late hand.

There are three illuminated capitals, one at the beginning of each part of the sermon, and a third on fol. 185ᵛ where the introduction ends and the sermon proper begins. Other majuscules are scattered in the text; some proper names are capitalized. Punctuation consists of periods and reversed semicolons. Occasional words and lines are underlined.

Rarely is an abbreviation used. Marginal references are found both in the hand of the sermon and in a later hand. A late hand has added occasional words omitted from the text. On folio 193ʳ a reading, "þat he stank so foule þat he was heuy þerwiþ and myȝt now suffre it," has been omitted; the line has been left blank.

The incipit, written in a late hand, reads: "This sermoun suynge was prechid atte Poulis crosse at two tymes of Maistrer Thomas Wymbiltoun in the ȝeer of oure lord a þousand þree hundrid foure score and eiȝte."

Rb—B. M. Royal MS. 18 B xxiii

British Museum. See Warner and Gilson, I, xxxi; II, 396; Wells, *Manual*, Fourth Supplement, p. 1266; Eighth Supplement, p. 1669. *Middle English Sermons, Edited from British Museum MS. Royal 18 B xxiii*, edited by Woodburn O. Ross, EETS, no. 209 (London, 1940) (Contains forty-seven of the English sermons in this manuscript).

Paper; with the outer and inner leaves of quire vi, last leaf of quire vii and f. 174 vellum; 11½ x 8¼ inches; 174 folios; middle of the fifteenth century.

Contents:

Homilies and Sermons, in *Latin* and *English*, viz:—

1. Seventeen Latin homilies, chiefly exegetical, on the Sunday gospels, Advent—1st Sund. after the Octave of Epiphany.	f. 1
2. *Latin* sermon in another hand on Matt. xv. 13.	f. 21
3. Seventeen short *Latin* sermons on various festivals. The series is interrupted (f. 27ᵇ) by some theological commonplaces and (f. 28ᵇ) the common mythical statistics of parishes, etc., in England. . . . At the end is a table of sermons in art. 1, 3.	f. 24
4. Sermon (in two parts) in *English* (by Thomas Wimbledon).	f. 39
5. Forty-four sermons in *English*, not arranged in any consistent scheme, though certain groups evidently hang together. There is no name of author, and the difference of styles may indicate that they are by several authors. The first and last and one other, however, are certainly by John Myrcus or Mirk, prior of Lilleshall.	f. 49
6. Sermons for 5th-7th Sundays after Trinity.	f. 150
7. General table, with short heads, in *Latin*, of the sermons in art. 5, 6, 8.	f. 159
8. Sermons, resembling some of those in art. 5.	f. 166

Ownership: The manuscript can be traced to the library of John Lord Lumley (1534?—1609). After Lumley's death, James I purchased the library for Henry, Prince of Wales. It remained in the Royal library until that library was incorporated in the British Museum by the Act of 1753 (Warner and Gilson, I, xviii-xix, xxxi-xxxii).

Wimbledon's Sermon: There are no missing pages; however, the scribe has abridged the sermon by omitting explanatory passages; the following lines are missing: 206-237; 246-307; 350-385.

From 33 to 38 lines are found on a page. The ink has faded on some of the pages, but the letters are still legible. The pagination has been done by a late hand.

Although a space has been left for the illumination of the initial *R* of *Redde,* the letter has not been supplied. Majuscules begin certain sentences and proper names, but there is no illumination whatsoever. Punctuation consists of double vertical lines and of periods. Words and phrases are often underlined. Each small section of the sermon begins on a new line, a practice which often leaves the preceding line half blank.

The marginalia are in the same hand as the text. The scribe employs many abbreviations. Only a very few words are inserted above the line, and none are added or changed in the margin. Occasionally the scribe has cancelled an incorrect word, and immediately following has written it correctly.

There is no rubric attributing the sermon to Wimbledon. At the end of the sermon, in the same hand, is inscribed: "Thomas Looke." This signature, according to Ross, also follows other sermons, six Latin and seventeen English, including Mirk's. Ross intimates that the signature is puzzling, especially since the sermons are written in various hands; as a possible explanation he suggests that this manuscript has been copied from another whose scribe was Thomas Looke (Ross, *Middle English Sermons*, xvi).

S—Cambridge, Sidney Sussex, MS. 74

Sidney Sussex Library, Cambridge. See M. R. James, *A Descriptive Catalogue of the Manuscripts in the Library of Sidney Sussex College, Cambridge* (Cambridge, 1895), pp. 52-53. Wells, *Manual*, Fourth Supplement, p. 1266; Brown, *Register*, I, 234; II, 236.

Vellum; 10⅛ x 7 inches; 207 folios; dated by the catalogue as fifteenth century (?).

Contents:

Sermons . . .	f. 1
A treatise upon the Pater Noster.	f. 143
Redde rationem villicationis tue.	f. 168
Exposition of the X Commandments.	f. 181
Exposition of Ave Maria.	f. 189b
Six sermons in three different hands.	f. 191b

Ownership: The manuscript was given to the Sidney Sussex Library by Dr. Samuel Ward, Master of Sidney Sussex College, before his death in 1643.

Wimbledon's Sermon: The text is complete, although the reading is difficult to decipher because of blotches or fading of the ink. From 37 to 39 lines are found on a page. A worn place, like a thumb print, on the edge of the manuscript, has obscured a few marginal notes. The pagination was done by an early hand.

The beginning letter of each of the two parts of the sermon is illuminated in red and blue. Other non-illuminated capitals follow the paragraph marks. The incipit, "Redde rationem villicationis tue. Luce," is in red ink. The only mark of punctuation is a light vertical line.

There are few abbreviations. Marginal references are both in the same hand as the text and in a later hand. Many textual omissions have been added in a later hand. This hand has cancelled some words and inserted others; for example, *rekenyng* has been cancelled and *dome* written in the margin (f. 169ʳ); for *þerfor*, *Loo what* has been written (f. 171ʳ). Other words have been glossed, e.g., *churles* as *chinches*, *louuere* as *ruler*, *rauind* as *reven*.

On page 167 opposite the first page of the sermon, a late hand has written: "A Sermon no laser (*sic*) godlie then learned preached at Paules crosse, on the Sondayes Quinquagesima, Anno Mccclxxxix by R. Wymbleton." Another late hand has written at the end of the sermon (f. 180ᵛ): "Explicit sermo factus et compilatus per maiesterum Thomam Wymbeldon."

T—Cambridge, Trinity College, MS. 322

Trinity College Library, Cambridge. See M. R. James, *The Western Manuscripts in the Library of Trinity College, Cambridge* (Cambridge, 1900) pp. xxiii, 437-438. Wells, *Manual*, Sixth Supplement, p. 1449; Brown, *Register*, I, 235; II, 236.

Vellum; 7¼ x 4¾ inches; ff. 4 + 180; dated by the catalogue as fourteenth, fifteenth century.

Contents:

1. 'Some English Homilies of yᵉ Epistles & Gospels in which are several things agˢᵗ the pope, by Wickliffe as I believe.   f. 1
2. Redde rationem villicacionis tue.   f. 242
3. "A Pious treatise which beginneth thus: In euere syngul man and woman þat is bounde in dedely synne beþ þre wrychydnes.   f. 274
4. On the Pater Noster.   f. 148ᵇ
5. (Bonventura's) Meditations on the Passion.   f. 150ᵇ

Ownership: The manuscript was given to Trinity College by John Whitgift, Archbishop of Canterbury, who from 1567 to 1577 was Master of Trinity College.

Wimbledon's Sermon: The text is not complete. Like *Hr* and *P*, the other two manuscripts in Group *b*,[6] lines 764-1026 are missing. Also the folio between pages 249 and 250 has been torn out; thus lines 183-235 are missing.

The numbering has been done by two hands; one has foliated and the other, paginated. Often the pagination obscures the foliation, or

[6]See "Chapter III: Relationship of Manuscripts. A. English Manuscripts," p. 27.

vice versa. Some words are obscured by the binding. Page 242 is a palimpsest. There are from 26 to 31 lines on a page.

The first letter of the sermon is illuminated. Other non-illuminated capitals follow the paragraph marks, which are few in number. Colons and periods are used for punctuation. The incipit and explicit are in the same hand, but in different ink. Some words are underlined.

The usual abbreviations are found. The marginalia, consisting of references and inserts, are in the same hand as the sermon.

A rubric, written by a later hand, in the margin of the first page of the sermon (p. 242) reads: "A sermon preach'd at Paul's Cross, A.D. 1389, by Tho. Wymbleton on Quinquagesima Sunday." The explicit at the end is in the same hand as the sermon but in different ink. It reads (p. 293): "Thomas Wymbyldon istum composuit sermonem at crucem S. pauli london, qui obiit in die omnium sanctorum amen. Ricardi tercii, con(qu)estum xv. cuius anime propicietur deus. Amen."

U—Oxford, University College, MS. 97

University College Library, Oxford. See Henricus O. Coxe, *Catalogus Codicum MSS. qui in Collegiis Aulisque Oxoniensibus Hodie Adservantur* (2 pts., Oxford, 1852), Part I, 28-29; Wells, *Manual*, Seventh Supplement, p. 1571.

Codex membranaceus; quarto; 185 folios; fifteenth century.

Contents:

1. De prophetia Sancti Thomæ de Canturbyry; Anglice. — f. 1
2. Prophetia Henrici prophetæ. — p. 4
3. Gesta Romanorum moralizata. — p. 9
4. Calixti papæ III. bulla ad Thomam Bourchier, archiep. Cantuar. de bello Dei contra Infideles; dat. 1456. — p. 161
5. Prophetiæ de nomine regis qui Sanctam Crucem inveniret. — p. 164
6. Medicina contra fluxum et pro stigmate. — p. 166
7. Exposition on the Ten Commandments (by Hampole?), — p. 169
8. Here bigynnen the vii. commaundements of the New Testament.
9. Here begynneth how men that been in heele schuld visite seeke folke. — p. 186
10. Postil on 'Thou schalt love thi Lord, thi God, of al thyn herte.' — p. 193
11. Excerptum ex S. Bernardi Florum viij. capitulo quadragesimo quinto. — p. 195
12. Bernardi Senensis epistola ad Raimundum dominum Castri Ambrosii, de cura rei familiaris. — p. 196
13. Two sermons upon Luc. xvi. 'Redde racionem villicationis tue.' — p. 201
14. This tretis next folewynge maade sir Johan Clanevowe, kny3t, the laste viage that he maade ouer the greete see in whiche he dyede; of whos soul Jhesu haue mercy. — p. 227
15. An exposicioun of the Pater noster, in schort. — p. 246
16. The twelve articles of the feith. — p. 249
17. Heere bigynneth a sentence ful good and profitable to rede, which is icleped the Myrour of synneres, (by Hampole.) — p. 253
18. A meditacion of the fyue woundes of Crist. — p. 262
19. A trete that Richard hermyte maade to a good ankeresse that he louede. — p. 266

Ownership: Coxe states that the manuscript was formerly in the chapel of St. Peter of Westminster, where Blanche, Duchess of Lancaster was buried. It was given to University College Library c. 1664 by Thomas Walker, master of University College.

Wimbledon's Sermon: The text is complete. The pagination has been done by two hands, both rather late. There are 41 or 42 lines on a page.

No letter is illuminated, although the capitals of the major sections are in red ink; the *R* or *Redde* and the *M* of *My*, on the first page of the sermon, are slightly larger than the others. Both the paragraph marks and the vertical lines used for punctuation are in red ink. Some few words and lines are underlined. The few marginal references are in the same hand as the sermon.

2. LATIN MANUSCRIPTS

There are two Latin versions of the sermon: Cambridge, Gonville and Caius MS. 334—G; and Cambridge, University Library MS. Ii III 8—Ul. Neither Latin manuscript can be the original: the Gonville and Caius MS. has quotations translated from the English; the University Library MS. has far too many omissions to be the original.[7] Descriptions of these two manuscripts follow.

G—Cambridge, Gonville and Caius MS. 334

Gonville and Caius College Library, Cambridge. See M. R. James, *A Descriptive Catalogue of the Manuscripts in the Library of Gonville and*

---

[7]See "Chapter III: Relationship of Manuscripts. B. The Latin Manuscripts," p. 32.

Caius College (Cambridge, 1907), I, viii, 376-377; Wells, *Manual*, Fourth Supplement, p. 1266; *DNB*, s. v. "William Moore."

Vellum; 10⅞ x 8¼ inches; ff. 198 + 6; fourteenth and fifteenth centuries.

Contents:

1. Sermons . . .	f. 1
2. Seneca (martinus Dumiensis) de quatuor uirtutibus.	f. 8ᵇ
3. Inc. sentencie quorundam philosophorum.	f. 10
4. Redde rationem villicationis tue (Latin).	f. 10ᵇ
5. Tabula super Thomam de Veritate Theologica.	f. 19
6. S. Thomas . . . de Veritate Theologica.	f. 24
7. Joh. Waldeby super orationem Dominicam.	f. 112
8. Idem (?) super *Aue Maria*.	f. 136ᵇ
9. Idem super articulos fidei.	f. 150
10. Eiusdem (?) Sermones (14).	f. 172ᵇ

Ownership: A fifteenth century hand has written on folio 198ᵛ: "Iste liber constat henrico Groome clerico." On this same folio, as well as on a flyleaf at the beginning is a note, dated June 25, 1627, stating that the volume also belonged to John Causton, Rector of Clopton Oteley in Suffolk. The manuscript is one of 150 volumes bequeathed in 1659 to Gonville and Caius Library by William Moore, librarian of Cambridge University Library.

Wimbledon's Sermon: The text is complete; stains at the corners of several folios do not affect the text. There are 40 lines on a page. Lines for the writing as well as those for the margin are visible.

The beginning *R* of *Redde* is illuminated. Other capitals, in proper names and at the beginning of sentences, are not illuminated. There are a few paragraph marks in a different ink.

Many abbreviations are used, both for endings of words and for whole words, as *quam, quod, quae, quia, esse, scilicet*. The references, which in the English versions are found in the margin, are in the Latin versions incorporated in the text itself. Except for one word, which is an insertion, the marginalia are all in a later hand. These usually refer to the content of the sermon, as "3 questiones," "quomodo intrasti," or "secundus ballinus."

A late hand has written just preceding the sermon: "Author R. Wimbledon, Exeat Anglice."

Ul—Cambridge, University Library MS. Ii III 8

University Library, Cambridge. See *A Catalogue of the Manuscripts Preserved in the Library of the University of Cambridge* (5 v., Cambridge, 1858), III, 411-412; Wells, *Manual*, Fourth Supplement, p. 1266. G. R. Owst, *Preaching in Medieval England* (Cambridge, 1926), 362.

Paper; 170 folios; fourteenth century.

Contents:

1. 'Tractus de decem Mandatis per utilis valde'.	f. 1
2. 'Tractatus compendiosus de decem mandatis'.	f. 13[b]
3. 'Tractatus de decem mandatis etc.'	f. 18[b]
4. 'Tractatus de decem mandatis'.	f. 31[b]
5. 'Ars Predicandi'.	f. 37
6. Sermons in three different hands.	f. 41

Wimbledon's Sermon:

Although there are many sections omitted from this Latin text, there is no folio missing. There are from 35 to 36 lines on a page. Certain letters are blurred by ink blots, but otherwise the text is in good condition.

There are no letters illuminated, but at the beginning of each of the two parts there is a blank space with a small letter notation for the illuminator. The incipit, paragraph marks, and capitals, which begin some sentences, are in red. Occasional phrases and words are underlined with red ink. Vertical lines, periods, and reversed semicolons are all used for punctuation.

As in *G*, there are many abbreviations both for syllables and for words: e.g. *is, ri, er, ra, ur, . . ibus, . . cionem, quod, que, quem, quoniam, quia, quid, post, etiam, et, enim, ille.* Also like *G*, references to sources are found in the text proper. Except for one notation, marginalia are in the hand of the scribe of the sermon. Occasionally the scribe has expunged an incorrect word, and then has written it correctly.

Owst states that all the sermons in the University Library manuscript are written in the same vigorous style; he therefore suggests that Thomas Wimbledon may be the author of the entire collection. However, from the evidence it would seem that Wimbledon originally wrote the sermon in English; certainly, as Owst says, English was the original language of delivery.[8]

3. ANALYSIS OF CONTENTS OF MANUSCRIPTS

The contents of the manuscripts which contain "Redde Rationem" are predominantly homiletical or devotional. The Church and religion were an important part of medieval life, and religious writing constitutes a significant portion of medieval literature. However, even where the primary concern of a work is not religious, a moral purpose is dis-

[8]Owst, *Preaching in Medieval England*, pp. 362, 230. See "Chapter III: Relationship of Manuscripts. B. The Latin Manuscripts," p. 32.

cernible; poets as well as preachers made use of devotional material. Hence the manuscripts are of the sort appropriate both for the libraries of preachers and other religious writers and also for medieval libraries in general.

Ht contains only Wimbledon's sermon plus two pages from a Latin missal. Homilies written for particular Sundays during the year are found in *Ra* and *Rb;* other anonymous sermons, with no particular designation, form a part of *G, Ul, Rb,* and *S; S* contains a number of Lollard treatises. A few sermons or treatises are attributed to particular writers; e. g. one sermon in *A* and several in *T* to Wycliff; a treatise in *A* to Richard de Wethershed and another to Richard Alkartoun; a treatise in *A* to John Mirk. *H2* contains only Wimbledon's sermon and sermons by "venerabili magistro Johanne Quintano." *Hu, Hr,* and *P* contain prayers of various sorts. In *Ul* is found a tract on the art of preaching.

The following works found in the manuscripts are rather interesting:

S. Thomas de Veritate Theologica, *G*
Excerptum ex S. Bernardi Florum, *U*
Gesta Romanorum, *U*
Translation of part of the Somme Le Roi of Frere Laurent, *A*

Although I have been unable to identify the "de Veritate Theologica," its author, "S. Thomas," is presumably St. Thomas Aquinas. The treatise may have been a part of his *Summa Theologiae*, a monumental work of theology and scholastic philosophy.

"Excerptum ex S. Bernardi Florum" is presumably a part of *Flores seu Sententiae ex S. Bernardi operibus depromptae*. Bernard's Flores contains about one hundred and seventy-five quotations from his writings, and would have been useful to the preacher in the preparation of his sermons or to any writer in search of devotional material.

Gesta Romanorum was a popular collection of stories to be used as exempla in sermons; the stories exist solely for the sake of moralization, and are themselves of little importance. There is often only a slight connection between the story and the moral.

Several middle English translations of Friar Lorens' *Le Somme lei Roi* (or *Le Somme des Vices et des Vertues*) are extant. Michel's *Ayenbite of Inwit* is one; another has been edited by W. Nelson Francis.[9] The books contained the following six parts: 1. Ten Commandments, 2. Apostles' Creed, 3. Seven Deadly Sins, 4. Treatise on Death, 5. Pater Noster, 6. Seven Gifts of the Holy Spirit.

The following works, written or ascribed to Richard Rolle, are scattered among the manuscripts:

[9]*The Book of Vices and Virtues*, EETS, no. 217 (London, 1942).

Form of Perfect Living, *Hu*
The Mirror, *U, P*
The Three Grades of Love, *P*
Commandment of the Love of God, *P*

Meditations on the following subjects occur in more than one manuscript:

Ave Marie, *G, S*
Pater Noster, *G, T, S, Hr* (2), *P,U*
Ten Commandments, *Ul, S, Hr, U* (Hampole?)
Articles of Faith, *G, U*
On the Passion, *Hr, P* (2), *T* (Bonaventura)
The three arrows to be shot on Doomsday, *U, P*
A short rule of life for priests, lords, and laborers, *H9, Hr*
How men in health should visit sick men, *Hr, U*

There are a few isolated tracts in *G* and *U* on subjects other than religious. The moral nature of the tract in *G*, Seneca on the Four Virtues, explains its inclusion with homeletical treatises. In addition to devotional tracts, *U* contains an interesting variety of material, including the four following:

Chronicle from A.D. 140 to 1382
Chronicle from beginning of the world to 1399
Account of a voyage made by Sir John Clanevowe
Will of Robert Folkyngham, Dec. 3, 1399

However, in general, sermons and devotional treatises manifest the type of subject matter assembled in these manuscripts.

B. THE PRINTS

See A. W. Pollard, G. W. Redgrave, et. al., *A Short-Title Catalogue of Books Printed in England, Scotland, and Ireland, and of English Books Printed Abroad, 1475-1640* (London, 1946), p. 601; *Catalogue of Books in the Library of the British Museum Printed in England, Scotland, and Ireland, and of Books in English Printed Abroad to the Year 1640* (3 v., London, 1884), II, 1612; *Early English Printed Books in the University Library Cambridge (1475-1640)* (4 v., Cambridge, 1900), II, 1764; IV, 575; *Notes and Queries, Sixth Series*, XI (April 18, 1885), 305; XI (May 9, 1885), 372-373; Joseph Ames, et. al., *Typographical Antiquities* (4 v., London, 1810-1819), II, 746, 1093, 1030, 1105; III, 1317; IV, 317, 339, 459, 563, 569; Wells, *Manual*, Fourth Supplement, p. 1266; Seventh Supplement, p. 1614.

The number of early printed editions of the sixteenth and seventeenth centuries attests to its popularity. The following list enumerates these editions and gives the present known locations of each.

R. Kele (1550?)*—2 editions—Emmanuel College, Cambridge; St. Paul's Cathedral Library; Folger Library

J. Awdely, 1572—St. Paul's Cathedral Library

J. Awdely, 1573—Bodleian Library

J. Awdely, 1575—British Museum; Bodleian Library; Folger Library; Huntington Library; St. Paul's Cathedral Library

J. Charlewood, 1578—British Museum

J. Charlewood, 1579—British Museum; Bodleian

J. Charlewood, 1582—British Museum; Huntington Library; Folger Library; St. Paul's Cathedral Library

J. Charlewood, 1584—British Museum; Bodleian Library; Folger Library; St. Paul's Cathedral Library

J. Charlewood, 1588—British Museum; Folger Library

J. Charlewood, 1593—Bodleian Library

J. Roberts, 1593—British Museum; Folger Library

J. Roberts 1603—St. Paul's Cathedral Library

W. Jaggard, Eleventh edition, 1617—British Museum; Folger Library; Yale University Library

W. Jaggard, Twelfth edition, 1617—Cambridge University Library; St. Paul's Cathedral Library

T. Cates and R. Cates, Thirteenth edition, 1629—British Museum

T. Cates, Fourteenth edition, 1634—British Museum; Huntington Library

T. Cates, Fifteenth edition, 1635—British Museum; Folger Library

Redde rationem is also bound with several other sermons in a book which belonged to T. Tanner (Tanner 832 (4)), now found in the Bodleian Library. The title page of this edition is missing, but the catalogue suggests that this copy is probably the 1584 edition above. It does correspond to the second group of prints, of which the 1584 edition is the first.[10]

Not only was the sermon published in these individual editions, but Owst states that the "Puritans were delighted to bind it up with their own volumes of sermons," even at times incorporating sections verbatim in a sermon presumably the writer's own (Lincoln Cathedral Library MS. A. 6. 2, ff. 67^b-70; 217-end).[11] It is found in two notable collections, the best known being Foxe's *Acts and Monuments*, first published in 1562.[12] In the eighteenth century it reappeared in *Phoenix Britannicus*, which is defined by its sub-title as being a "Miscellaneous Collection of Scarce and Curious Tracts, Historical, Political, Biographical, Satirical, Critical, Characteristical, etc, Prose and Verse, only to be found in the Cabinets of the Curious Interspersed with Choice Pieces from Original MSS."[13] The editor said of his volume:

* Not examined.

[10]See third paragraph below.

[11]Owst, *Preaching in Medieval England*, p. 361; note 5, p. 361.

[12]John Foxe, *Actes and Monuments* (Imprinted at London by John Day dwellyng over Aldergate cum privilegio Regie Majestatis, 1563), pp. 175-183.

[13]*Phoenix Britannicus*, collected by J. Morgan, Gent. (London: Printed for the Compiler, and T. Edlin, at the Princes' Arms against Exeter Exchange in

In this go some Phoenixes, which I am almost positive very few now living have
ever seen, even in Catalogues.

Redde rationem was the first selection, printed in its first issue in January, 1731.

The 16th and 17th century prints are generally small octavo volumes,
with an occasional quarto, duodecimo, or sextodecimo. The prints
examined are in good condition with the exception of the Bodleian copy
of the 1573 Awdeley and the Tanner, both of which have missing pages.
Most of the bindings are late—18th or 19th century; some of the editions are bound separately, but many of them are found bound with
other sermons, printed at various times.

The prints fall roughly into two groups. The first, the 1573 and 1575
Awdely and the first three Charlewood editions, are printed on 48
leaves, signatures A^8-F^8; the 1572 Awdely text corresponds page for
page with this same group, 48 leaves, but with 12 signatures A^4-L^4. The
second group, Charlewood 1582 through the fifteenth edition by T.
Cates, contains 32 leaves, 4 signatures A^8-D^8. The editions of Group I
and those in Group II agree with others in the particular group. Occasionally obsolete or questionable words have been amended or the
phrasing slightly altered.

The title pages of Group I are decorated by a single border, while
those of Group II are plainer. The first group designate the work as

A Sermoun no lesse fruteful then famous. Made in the year of our Lrd God
M.C.lxxxviii and founde out hyd in a Wall.

Which sermon is here set forth by the old copy, without adding or diminishing
saue the old and rude English here and there amended.

Later editions, those of Group II, Foxe, and *Phoenix Britannicus*, repeat
this designation; and those in Group II add the fact that the sermon
was preached at Paul's Cross on Quinquagesima Sunday by "R. Wimbledon in the raigne of King Henrie the fourth."

The editorial notes introducing the sermon show that it was highly
regarded. Awdeley included an address to the reader, which was printed
in the succeeding prints and in the *Phoenix Britannicus:*

Loe, Christian reader, while the worlde not slumbred, but routed and snorted
in the deepe and dead sleepe of ignorancie, some lyuelye spirites were wakynge,
and ceased not to call uppon the drousy multitude of men, and to styrre them up

the Strand; and J. Wilford, at the Three Golden Flower de Luces, behind the
Chapter-House, St. Paul's, 1731-1732), I, 1-17.

(Each selection printed for the *Phoenix Britannicus* appeared separately and
sold for 15s.; it could be procured by subscription or at "Will's Coffee House,
opposite the Admiralty.")

from the long dreames of sinful living, that once at the last they wold creepe out of darknes, and come forth to the hot shining sunne of Gods worde, that both the filthe mistes of their hartes might be driven away, and also their heavy and dying spirites recreated, refreshed and quickned. So that no man can alledge that in any age there wanted Preachers of Gods word: For he that keepeth Israel sleepeth not, ne slumbreth. And though thorowe his secrete counsayl, he sendeth more labourers into his harvest at one time then at another, yet he hath euer some to weede, to reape, to gather shraues together into the harnes of euerlasting life. Reade therefore diligently thys litle Sermon so long sithens writen, and thou shalt perceive the same quicke spirite in the authour therof that thou now marvellest at in other of our time. He sharply, earnestly, and wittely rebuketh the syns of all sortes of men, and speaketh as one hauying authoritia, and not as the Scribes and Pharises, which with their leaden and blount dartes could neuer touch the quicke, though they haue occupied, and worne the pulpites so many yeares. The woord of God is lyuelye, and mightie in operation, and sharper then any two edged swoorde, and cutteth euen unto the division of the soule, and of the spirite, and of the joyntures and mary etc. Wherefore eftsoones I exhort thee to reade this little treatise diligently, and not onlye to reuerence antiquitie, and the lyuely spirite, and word of God therein, but also to learne, both to acknowledge and moreover to amende the wyckednes of thy lyfe which God graunt for his Cristes sake.

In the eighteenth century the editor of *Phoenix Britannicus* defends his choice of the sermon as the first selection to be printed:

In order to make a good Beginning, I chuse to set out with a Sermon: but such a one as must be allowed to be no less remarkable for its Contents (considering the Time of Day it was wrote in, the Year after the Death of our famous Reformer John Wickliff) than venerable for its Antiquity. As it boldly points out to every Steward his respective Duty, the same may, perhaps, be full as necessary to be known in these our still later Times, as the anonymous Publisher deemed it to be when he first communicated it in Print. He unluckily omitted informing when that was; but some good Judges, to whom I have shewed it, are, by its Aspect, of Opinion, that it may claim a Place among the earliest Products of the English Printing Presses.

Some of the eighteenth century Anglican readers of the *Phoenix Britannicus* were troubled by the Catholic content of the sermon. But the editor satisfactorily answers the criticism in a Postscript to the Preface (I, ii):

Bless us! How can this be? I am quite at a Loss to conceive why it should. The Pens of ingenious Romanists entertain me as agreeably as those of any others, and doubtless will do the like to at least some of my Readers; and why may they not therewith be gratified? Besides; how can any of us well take Exceptions at Extracts given us from writings of approved Authors of our oun Belief?

In short, once for all, I would be understood to be absolutely a Neuter in Party Affairs: But shall not fail of reviving what I judge will best take of my Readers.

Certainly one of these readers was pleased, for in a letter to the editor he praises the work (I, 22):

The antique Style and Spelling, notwithstanding your Editor's then-modern Corrections; the Date of but one Year from Wickliffe's Death, who, tho' he had some Followers, had but few Equals; the Clearness of Thought; the regular Disposition of suitable Ideas; the Vivacity of Wit; the Firmness of Judgement; the general String of Learning, much above that miserable Age; the sound Divinity;

the simple and honest Piety; the noble Boldness; the virtuous Spirit of Reforma-
tion; the Unworldliness of Mind; the Evangelical Attachment to Sacred Scrip-
ture; the no Regard for jugling Traditions; the never requiring implicit Credulity,
without rational Bases; lastly the common Enmity of most priesthod to these
amiable Qualifications, etc. do all of them concur, in almost demonstrating
John Wickliffe to be the sole probable Author of so admirable a Sermon; nor is
it, from such evident Marks, much doubted by
                                             Your humble servant.

Foxe, in his first edition, also attributes the sermon to Wyclif (p .175):

It seemeth to be of Wickliffe's doing, but whether it be or not, no doubt it
sauoureth of that time, and for the frute thereof most worthy to come in amongst
thother actes of these good men.

In the second and following editions Foxe acknowledges it as R. Wimbledon's sermon.

Just as the number of manuscripts attests to the widespread popularity
of the sermon during medieval times, so the number of printed editions
and the comments made by readers would indicate a continued interest
during later centuries.

Chapter III

RELATIONSHIP OF THE MANUSCRIPTS

A. ENGLISH MANUSCRIPTS

The English texts are widely divergent. Only two groups of manuscripts are unequivocally related: Group *b*—*H9*, *Hr*, *P*, *T;* Group *c*—*A*, *H2*. Several of the other manuscripts have a few similar passages, but there is not enough evidence to establish a close relationship.

Eleven of the thirteen English manuscripts examined have many individual variants; therefore, each of the eleven is obviously unsuitable as a basic text. *Ht*, the manuscript edited by Sundén, is one of the most anomalous. *C* has the smallest number of individual variants; hence, in this edition, it is selected as the basic text.

Whenever a reading of a manuscript (or of a few manuscripts) differs from that of all the other manuscripts, this reading is a variant. Since a variant once inserted in a manuscript is likely to be reproduced whenever that manuscript is transcribed, by the comparison of like variants the relationship of the manuscripts is established. Only significant variants, consisting of omissions, additions, and wholly different wordings, are considered. Minor differences of wording and order, though frequently found, are not so significant.

Although a variant, once established, is likely to be transcribed, each variant ultimately can be attributed to a scribe; each originates either from a scribal error in copying or from scribal editing. Some scribal errors are due to ignorance: the scribe, not knowing the original word, may substitute another; other errors are caused by eyeskip between identical words, by the transcription of the wrong letter or word, or by other forms of carelessness. In editing a text, a scribe may deliberately add, change, or omit words or phrases.

The frequency and importance of similar variants in Group *b* (*H9*, *T*, *Hr*, *P*) indicate that these four manuscripts form a group and stand together against the others. The relationship can be thus depicted:

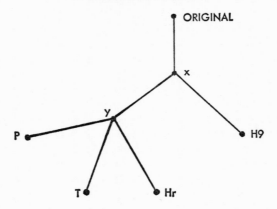

The following are the significant readings which *H9*, *T*, *Hr*, *P* have in common and in which they deviate from almost all the other manuscripts:

Additions: 88, 90, 155, 156, 181, 314-315, 451, 497, 585, 669, 710, 711, 713, 719, 732, 756, 1070
Changes of words: 46, 298, 438, 440, 592, 734, 1061, 1067, 1094, 1102
Omissions: 178, 181-182, 312, 312-313, 349, 438, 506, 600

From this evidence it is clear that *H9*, *Hr*, *T*, and *P* descend from a common ancestor *x*.

H9 agrees with the other manuscripts in more readings than *T*, *P*, and *Hr;* therefore *H9* must be closer to the original than *T*, *Hr*, or *P*. In the following readings, *H9* agrees with the majority reading where *T*, *Hr*, and *P* deviate from it:

Additions: 14, 21, 60, 89, 104, 124, 249, 251, 263, 277, 339, 400, 417, 513, 604, 609, 663, 692, 1056
Changes of words: 32, 39, 52, 70, 81, 94, 138, 166, 245, 298, 346, 382, 420, 455-456, 525, 539, 599, 626, 634, 641-642, 647, 678-679, 1056, 1056-1057, 1057, 1065, 1074, 1082, 1088
Omissions: 24, 33, 59, 163, 164, 239, 250, 349, 397-398, 550, 577, 610, 632, 739-740, 764-1026, 1030-1031, 1058

These variations in *T*, *Hr*, and *P* prove the close relationship of these three manuscripts.

Certain omissions, changes, and additions in *H9* not found in *T*, *Hr*, and *P*, show that *H9* cannot be the source of *T*, *Hr*, and *P*. In the following readings *H9* deviates from *T*, *Hr*, and *P*, and from all other manuscripts except *Rb;* the variants that *Rb* and *H9* have in common are marked with an asterisk.

Additions: 41, 81, 186, 245, 409*, 454*, 574*, 727*, 735*, 736*, 788*, 818, 830*, 891

Changes of words: 89, 115, 400*, 419, 481*, 582, 587, 636*, 768, 1000

Omissions: 90-91*, 113, 158, 319-320, 329, 577, 623, 634, 663-665, 675-676, 738-740, 833, 865, 846-847, 886, 920-921, 1038

The variations of *T*, *Hr*, and *P* listed above in the second tabulation, indicate the close relationship of these three manuscripts. Since each possible pair of the three has variant readings where the third agrees with the majority reading, no one of the three can be the derivative of the other two, but the three must have a common ancestor *y*.

P and *T*
 Additions: 490, 605
 Changes of words: 86, 274, 309, 316-317, 342, 459, 606, 611, 694
 Omissions: 609-610
T and *Hr*
 Additions: 119
 Changes of words: 296, 665, 761, 1041
 Omissions: 1053
Hr and *P*
 Additions: 301, 1088
 Changes of words: 219†, 388
 Omissions: 232*, 234-235†

Each of these three manuscripts has a few variant readings peculiar to itself, though those of *T* are almost non-existent.

T
 Change of word: 121 (variation of this word is found in *P* also, along with the textual reading)
 Omissions: 183-235 (page of MS torn out), 338, 546-547
Hr
 Additions: 117, 532, 662
 Changes of words: 210, 509
 Omissions: 155, 265, 699
P
 Additions: 152, 168, 240, 256, 310, 342, 363, 546, 549, 623, 682, 744, 1079, 1090
 Changes of words: 13, 51, 99, 159, 208, 295, 338, 363, 365, 371, 428, 479, 524, 546-547, 547, 561
 Omissions: 42, 73, 108, 227, 441-442, 562, 586-587, 588-589, 620, 1064

Most of the variant readings, both with pairs and with individual manuscripts, are relatively simple. Of the three, *T* is the manuscript with the fewest number of individual variants. Aside from the omission of lines 183-235, caused by one page being torn from the Trinity MS., *T* has only three individual variants. However, the 15 variants that *P* and *T* have in

*Variant occurs also in *Rb*. Except for two other variants: an addition, 240, also found in *P*, and an omission, 312-313, also found in *Ht*, *P*, *Hr*, and *T*, the variants marked above are the only ones *H9* and *Rb* have in common; hence no close connection can exist between these two.

† Variant is a part of the text found on the page torn from *T*.

common would prevent *T* being the source of *Hr*. Likewise, the six variants of *T* and *Hr* make it doubtful that *T* was the source of *P*. There are three variants in *Hr* and *P* not found in *T*. Hence it cannot be proved that *T* is the source of either *Hr* or *P*, though the relationship of *T* with *P* seems closer than that of *T* with *Hr*. With the existing variants one can only affirm that the three, *T*, *P*, and *Hr*, had a common ancestor *y*.

Similar variants in *A* and *H2*, designated as Group *c*, show that these two manuscripts also are related and must descend from the common ancestor *z*.

The following are the significant readings which *A* and *H2* have in common and in which they deviate from other manuscripts.

> Additions: 203, 224, 249, 263, 270, 272, 308, 330, 414, 433, 451, 468, 473, 509, 529, 531, 532, 604, 817, 827, 1032, 1085
> Changes of words: 25, 71, 73, 105, 129, 273, 279, 395, 401, 404, 415, 417, 420, 475, 499, 531, 532, 578, 629, 630, 657, 777, 953, 1025, 1040
> Omissions: 51, 65, 72, 75, 259, 316, 344, 351, 366, 378, 431, 453, 505, 590-592, 622, 642-643, 778, 816, 817, 1017, 1078-1079, 1083

Aside from the above variants, there are a few variants peculiar to each manuscript:

> *H2* Variants:
> Additions: 65, 116
> Changes of words: 53, 69, 75, 287, 826, 1102
> Omissions: 82, 448, 450, 472, 816, 827, 1078-1079, plus the following due to defective MS:
> 668-774, 788-814, 828-986
> *A* Variants:
> Additions: 870*, 940*
> Changes of words: 672*, 698*, 744*, 793*, 796*, 910*, 933*
> Omissions: 84, 86, 186, 191, 225, 404, 689*, 728*, 867*, 873*, 886*, 1023-1024

Note in the above listing that many *A* variants are in sections missing in *H2;* however the few omissions left in *A* and the variants peculiar to *H2* negate the possibility of either being copied from the other, but certainly both must have been copied from the same manuscript.

A few variants of *A* and *H2*, not listed above, are found in *Rb* and *Ht*. However, as *Rb* and *Ht* do not have the many variants listed above as

---

*From section missing in *H2* because of torn manuscript.

peculiar to *A* and *H2*, *Rb* and *Ht* cannot be included in Group II. As a matter of interest the variants within these four are listed below:

> *A*, *Rb*, *Ht*, *H2* variants:
>   Change of word: 11
>   Omission: 530*
> *A*, *Ht*, *H2* variants:
>   Additions: 408, 521, 1073*
>   Changes of words: 6, 296, 478*, 630*
>   Omissions: 232-233, 305.
> *A*, *Rb*, *H2* variants:
>   Addition: 358*
>   Changes of words: 29, 70*, 173*, 243, 325
>   Omission: 111
> *A*, *Rb*, *Ht* variants:
>   Additions: 412*, 609*
>   Change of word: 754
> *A*, *Rb* variants:
>   Addition: 789 (*out H2*)
>   Omissions: 142, 939
> *Rb* and *Ht* variants:
>   Changes of words: 10*, 28*, 746*
>   Omissions: 312-313*, 602, 807, 960

The above variants are too few to establish a definite relationship.

Each manuscript has variants peculiarly its own. Not all the variants are listed here, but they are found in the critical apparatus accompanying the text. The number of individual variations in each manuscript (excluding Group *b: H9*, *P*, *T*, *Hr*, and Group *c: A*, *H2*) is given below; any variant found in two or more manuscripts is not counted.

MS.	Additions	Omissions	Change of word
Rb	66	76 plus 206-237 244-307	112
Ht	7	64	54
Hu	10	15 plus 117-153 302-339 1042-1102	6
U	8	8	19
S[1]	3	19	10
Ra	2	6	6
C	1	3	5

No one of the first five manuscripts in the preceding table (*Rb*, *Ht*, *Hu*, *U*, *S*) is suitable as a basic text; the individual variants are too many. Though the additions and word changes are more significant than the

---

*Variant also found in one or two other MSS.

[1]Some of the readings of *S* have been changed by a later hand. Many of the new readings agree with *H9* or with *T*, *Hr* and *H9;* others are peculiar to *S*.

omissions, all the variants need to be considered in the selection of the basic text.

From the preceding evidence, it is obvious that *Ht*, the manuscript edited by Sundén, is unsuitable as a basic text. Although it has only seven peculiar additions, in other ways it varies greatly from the other manuscripts. The number of word changes (54) and the number of omissions (64) indicate either that a careless scribe was editing the text or that the scribe was copying from a poor manuscript.

The selection of the basic text is between *Ra* and *C*, the two manuscripts with the fewest number of individual variants.[2] Of the two, *Ra* has the greater number of variants: if all the variants, insignificant as well as significant, are counted, *Ra* has 134 to *C*'s 126; *Ra* has 14 significant variants, while *C* has only 9; in common with one or more other manuscripts *Ra* has 8 variants while *C* has only 1.

Thus, of all the thirteen English manuscripts, *C* has the fewest significant omissions and is most free from editing and interpolations. Hence *C* must be nearest the original and is the manuscript chosen for the basic text.

B. THE LATIN MANUSCRIPTS

The two Latin texts: Cambridge, University Library MS. Ii III 8 (*Ul*) and Cambridge, Gonville and Caius MS. 334 (*G*), are independent Latin texts. *G* is obviously a translation of an English text. *Ul* may be a translation from an English text by a scribe more learned than the one who translated the *G* text, or *Ul* could be a transcription of a lost Latin text·

The Latin texts seldom coincide, for each has its own peculiar vocabulary and word order. Often the two texts merely use different Latin words; elsewhere *Ul* translates by one word, while *G* adds a synonym; there are 82 such synonyms in *G*. *G* follows the English word order and construction more closely than *Ul*. The differences in vocabulary and order can be seen in the following examples:

```
 5 seiþ on þis manere
     Ul ita ait
      G sic dicit
91-92 whanne þe day of his rekenyng comeþ þat is þe ende of þis lif
     Ul cum venerit dies compoti sui nox videlicet terminus vite
      G cum dies reddendi racionem villicacionis advenerit qui est fini huius
                 vite
21 in childhod
     Ul in infancia
      G in iuventute vel puericia
```

[2]Significantly, *Ra* and *C* have three important variants in common: 78, 361, 1005; it is possible that the two may be related in some way.

28 kuttyn awey
Ul resecant
G secant et amputant
123 baile
Ul ballinus
G ballinus vel villicus
78-80 it is nede þat summe beþ acremen, summe bakeris, summe makeris of
cloþ
Ul propterea oportet vt hic panem preparet illi, et ille texet isti
G oportunum est ut quidam sint coloni, quidam pistores, quidam
pannitores
128-130 y knowe no þyng þat shulde more drawe awey mannis vnresounable
loue fro þe passynge ioye of þis world þan þe mynde of þat dredful
rekenyng
Ul nichil vt nihi videtur magis excitat hominem ad retrahendi suum
illi citum amorem animalis huius seculi virtute transitorii quod
recordacio istius tremendi raciocinii
G nichil noverim quod magis subtraheret irrationabilem et indebitum
amorem hominum a transitorio gaudio huius mundi quam me-
moria illius tremendi iudicij

When a quotation is cited, the scribe of *Ul*, obviously the more edu-
cated man, usually transcribes the passage from the Latin source, or
sometimes merely gives the reference for the passage and omits the text;
on the other hand, the translator of *G* generally reconstructs the passage
in Latin from the English translation. Thus the two texts have altogether
different versions, as the following examples will show:

Ambrose, *De Nabuthiae:*[3] Nescit natura divites, quae omnes pauperes generat.
522-523 Kynde knowiþ no richessis, þat bryngeþ forþ alle men pore.
Ul Nescit natura divites que omnes pauperes generat.
G Natura non novit divitias que omnes homines giguit pauperes.

Gregory, *Moralium:*[4] Non autem debet hominum ducatum suscipere, que nescit
homines bene vivendo praeire.
381-382 He schal not take gouernayl of oþere þat cannot go byfore hem in
good lyuynge.
Ul Non debet hominum ducatum accipere qui nescit homines bene
vivendo praeire.
G Ipse non susciperet regimen aliorum qui nescit antecedere in bona
conuersatione.

Thus the differences in the two Latin versions give evidence of the in-
dependence of the two texts.

That *G* is a translation, not an original text, is clear from the nature
of the text; the number of synonyms for individual words, the Latin
vocabulary, and the order of the words—all point to the translation of *G*
from an English text.

Both the vocabulary and the word order of *Ul* could be those of an
original Latin Text. However, although *Ul* might possibly be a transcription of another Latin text which is lost, the unusual number of
variants would discount this text as the original of the English text.

[3]See Migne, *Patrologia Latina*, XIV, 770.
[4]See Migne, *PL*, LXXVI, 318.

The number of variants of the two manuscripts are listed below:

Ul
    Additions: 52
    Changes of words: 115
    Omissions: 234 plus 39-46, 69-78, 82-86, 216-224, 277-289, 448-454, 531-541, 610-617, 620-628, 683-686, 710-715, 837-901, 914-924, 940-950, 997-1002, 1097-1102
G Additions: 44 plus 82 synonyms
    Changes of words: 59
    Omissions: 62

The additions in *G* are individual words or phrases, while the additions in *Ul* range from words to sentences; some of the additions are as long as eight lines, and the majority range from one line to three.

This difference in *G* and *Ul* is also seen in the changes of words. Where individual words or phrases have been changed in *G*, whole paragraphs are often reworded in *Ul*. The scribe of *Ul* often condenses passages.

The number of omissions in *Ul* shows that *G* is the more nearly complete text. *G* omits only an occasional word of a passage in the English text; *Ul* omits many lines, paragraphs, and even pages. Some of these omissions in *Ul* cause serious breaks in thought; other omissions, consisting of passages of explication and proof, weaken the text.

These facts give evidence that *Ul* is not the original text.

Chapter IV

LANGUAGE OF CORPUS CHRISTI MS. 357

The dialect of the Corpus Christi text of "Redde rationem" is that of London in the latter part of the fourteenth century. The characteristics of this dialect[1] are repeatedly exemplified in the sermon, as the following lists indicate.

A. PHONOLOGY

1. The *i* mutation of *ă* plus a nasal becomes *ĕn*. The ME *en*-type is the regular Middlesex form, which influenced the Late London dialect. The Old City dialect, as that of Essex, has *an* instead of *en*. Although an occasional *an* survives in the Late London documents, it is not found in Wimbledon's sermon; here *en* is the only type, e.g. *men* 15, *fen* 616, *sendiþ* 644, *brenne* 555, *ende* 769.

2. OE *ǽ* becomes *ă* and occasionally *ĕ*. ME *ă* from OE *ǽ* is found in the Essex and Old City dialects; hence it survives in the Late London dialect and is exemplified in Wimbledon's sermon, e.g. *þat* 6, *what* 98, *was* 11, *hap* 168, *fadir* 240, *water* 461. From the Early Middlesex dialect a few *e*-forms survive in the Late London dialect; there are examples of the *e*-form in Wimbledon's sermon, e.g. *wheþer* 181, *wexenge* 22, *þer* 81.

The form *whodir* 736 is possibly explained by the influence of *w* on the vowel; *woþer wother* are given as variants in *NED*.

3. OE *ĕar* becomes *ăr* and occasionally *ĕr*. The *ar*-form in the Late London dialect survives from the Old City and Essex dialects; this is the predominant form in Wimbledon's sermon, e.g. *harme* 33, *hard* 245, *Godward* 691. The *er*-form, as *nerre* 823 in Wimbledon's sermon, is occasionally found in the Late London dialect, which probably absorbed it from the Early Middlesex dialect.

4. OE *ĕal* plus *d* becomes *ōld*, rarely *ēld*. The *eld*-form of the Old City, Early Middlesex, and Essex dialects rarely survives. The *old*-form, probably from the Buckinghamshire dialect, is practically the only one found

---

[1] See Barbara Alida Mackenzie, *The Early London Dialect* (Oxford, 1928), pp. 86–111; Henry Cecil Wyld, *A History of Modern Colloquial English* (London, 1920), pp. 49-59; Henry Cecil Wyld, *A Short History* of English (London, 1949); Richard Jordan, *Handbuch der Mittelenglischen Grammatik*, rev. by H. Ch. Matthes (Heidelberg, 1934); Joseph Wright and Elizabeth Mary Wright, *An Elementary Middle English Grammar*, Second edition (London, 1949).

in the Late London dialect and is the sole form found in Wimbledon's sermon, e.g. *old* 23, *folde* 261, *beholde* 353, *solde* 498, *cold* 541.

5. OE *ĕal* plus a consonant other than *d* becomes *ăll*. The *all*-form, a survival from the Old City and Essex dialects, is the sole form in the Late London dialect and in Wimbledon's sermon, e.g. *alle* 24, *falliþ* 39, *also* 47.

6. OE *ǣ*[1] (from W.G. *ai* plus *i* or *j*) and *ǣ*[2] (from W.G. *a*) become *ē* in the Late London dialect. In the twelfth and thirteenth centuries the OE *ǣ* had become *ā* in the Old City and Essex dialects. The *a*-type gradually gives way before the Middlesex type, *e*. Thus by the late fourteenth century, the *e*-type is the London form and is the one found in Wimbledon's sermon, e.g. *hest* 324, *rere* 421, *se* 453, *techeris* 43, *heete* 778, *weren* 53, *drede* 370, *gredynesse* 478, *dede* 506, *seed* 642, *lewid* 271.

The OE *ǣ* of both origins shortened to both *ă* and *ĕ*. The variants are either chronological or geographical. The *a* and *e* spellings occur side by side, often in the same word, as in Wimbledon's sermon: *any* 979, *eny* 32, *fatte* 261, *fettid* 36, *arst* 243, *erst* 415, *lat* 854, *lette* 41.

The *o* in *ony* 925 and *or* (ere) 168 is explained by Jordan; *ony* is explained by analogy to *ōn* (one); *or* is derived from the Old Norse *ār*.

7. OE *sĕl* usually remains *sĕl*, but occasionally becomes *sil*. The *sel*-type is a survival from the Old City and Essex dialects. The *sil*-form is explained by the fact that *e* was sometimes written *i* before *l*. Both forms are found in Wimbledon's sermon, e.g. *helle* 97, *dwelle* 99, *hymself* 140, *himsilf* 77, *sille* 514.

8. OE *ȳ* becomes *ī* (*ȳ*), *ĕ*, or *ŭ*. In the Old City and Essex dialects the *e*-form prevails, but both the *i*-form and the *u*-form are also found. In the Late London dialect the *i*-form, which prevails early in Middlesex, superseded the *e*-form; however, the *e*-form is still more prevalent than the *u*-form. All three forms are exemplified in Wimbledon's sermon, e.g. *first* 6, *myche* 120, *mynde* 390, *birdene* 616, *euyl* 117, *chirche* 207, *wiche* 215, *wheche* 325, *buryenge* 670, *biried* 671, *wermes* 696, *kynde* 17, *unkendely* 778, *cundelich* 596, *synnis* 40, *senful* 674, *suche* 224, *swiche* 290, *bysy* 887, *birþe* 896, *schit* 1055.

The *o* in *worst* 262 is the regular development of *u* after *w*.

9. OE o becoĕmes *ĕ*. Even in the Old English period the *ĕo* is monophthongized to *ĕ* in the Essex dialect, and this is taken over by the London area. The *e*-form is exemplified in Wimbledon's sermon, e.g. *erþe* 30, *heuene* 4, *herte* 159, *swerd* 40, *þeftes* 42, *werkis* 1020, *afeer* 520, *ferþe* 454, *cherlis* 274, *dere* 201, *sekenesse* 602, *werldly* 315, *derknesses* 829.

The *i*-spelling in *sik* 751 and in *dirknesses* 831 is explained by the position of the vowel before the palatal *k* and the *r*.

The forms *world* 16 and *worchyng* 848 are characteristic of West Midland; in the Midland areas and in Early Middlesex the *ĕo* was rounded to *ŏ*.

10. OE *i* mutation of *ĕa* becomes *ĕ*. This *e*-form survives from the Old City and Essex dialects and is exemplified in Wimbledon's sermon, e.g. *nede* 38, *elde* 595, *shewe* 131.

11. OE *i* mutation of *ɪo* becomes *ē*. In the Old City dialect the *i* mutation of *ɪo* becomes *ɪ̆*; this *i*-type in the Late London dialect is replaced by the *e*-type of East Midland; the *e*-type is found in Wimbledon's sermon, e.g. *dere* 2, *fend* 218, *herde* 240, *lese* 489.

12. OE *eag, eah* becomes *ey, egh, igh, ei, i*. The forms just listed are characteristic of Essex, West Midland, and Late London dialects and are exemplified in Wimbledon's sermon, e.g. *hiȝe* 181, *heye* 322, *heiȝere* 346, *eiȝen* 296, *eyȝe* 344, *nyȝe* 813.

13. Before *nd* all vowels were shortened; ME *ō* from OE *ā* remained *o* before nasals in the London and Southern dialects. The form is found in Wimbledon's sermon, e.g. *hond* 217, *lond* 43, *stondenge* 3.

B. MORPHOLOGY

1. Pronouns:

First person, nominative, singular is both *ich* and *I* in the Late London Dialect. The *I*-form is the more prevalent and is the form used in Wimbledon's sermon, where the common spelling is *y*.

Third person, plural, nominative is *þey. þey*, of Scandinavian origin, is found in all the fourteenth century London documents and is the pronoun used in Wimbledon's sermon.

Third person, plural, dative and accusative, is *hem. Hem*, from the OE dative *heom*, is the standard form in the Late London dialect. This is the form used in Wimbledon's sermon, with one exception, *hys* 405, a Southern and Kentish accusative form.

Third person, plural, genitive, is *here*, rarely *þeir. Here*, from the Old English genitive *heora*, is in general use in the Late London dialect and is the prevalent form in Wimbledon's sermon. In the fourteenth century, London documents begin to make use of the *þ*-forms of Scandinavian origin, coming through East Midland from the North. *þer* is occasionally found in Wimbledon's sermon.

2. Verbs:

The ending of the present indicative, singular, third person, is usually *eþ*, less frequently *iþ*. These endings, from the OE *eþ*, are the standard ones for the Late London dialect and are exemplified in Wimbledon's sermon, e.g. *clepeþ* 20, *clepiþ* 25, *falleþ* 44, *falliþ* 39, *accordeþ* 483, *acordiþ* 74, *likeþ* 218, *crieþ* 287.

There are two forms (present indicative, singular, third person) in the sermon which depart from the general rule: *stant* 383, which is a Southern and Kentish form; *kepet* 241, where the þ has become *t*.

The ending of the present indicative plural, is usually *eþ*, less frequently *en*. The Old City dialect preserved the *eþ* ending (OE *aþ*). Gradually the Midland ending *en* (OE subjunctive plural) eliminated the old *eþ* ending; by the end of the fourteenth century both endings are used in London and are exemplified in Wimbledon's sermon, e.g. *haueþ* 301, *hauen* 134, *comeþ* 208, *comen* 329, *beþ* 28, *ben* 31, *sykeþ* 203, *redeþ* 328. Occasionally in the Late London dialect *iþ*-ending is found; Wimbledon's sermon contains *etiþ* 504, *drediþ* 168, and *kuttyn* 28. There is also an archaic OE form in the sermon, *beoþ* 822.

The ending of the present participle is usually *-ynge*, less frequently *-enge*. The earlier *inde*-ending (from OE *ende*) of the Old City dialect has been displaced in the fourteenth century by the *inge*-ending from the South. The two endings, *-inge* and *-enge*, are exemplified in Wimbledon's sermon, e.g. *holdynge* 250, *sittynge* 447, *goynge* 423, *dwellynge* 471, *wexenge* 22, *ocupienge* 291. There is one exception in the sermon, *sittande* 291, which exemplifies the North and West Midland ending.

C. IRREGULAR FORMS

There are occasional irregular forms, which can be variously explained:

1. *Form from another dialect:*
   deie 50, 56—Midland form
   die 65—Southern form
   ȝouen 1020, 1028 (for pret. *ȝeuen*)—variant appears in Wycliff Bible, Gen. xiv, 33; possible influence of Old Norse *gǫ*
   saye 429 (for *saw*)—listed in NED as a variant in the 13th-16th centuries; *say* found in *Piers Plowman*, B, v. 9, 10
   oiþer 511—possible Northern form where OE *o* sometimes developed as *oy*
   ouþer 239—Southern form
   puple 49 *et al.*—Early London and Middlesex dialects; *peple*, the usual form, also found (122 *et al.*)
   drynge 817—[OE *drincan*]—similar form in Lambeth Homilies; *nk* sometimes became *ng*
2. *Development from etymon:*
   to wondry 272—regular development from the OE infinitive, *wundrian*, when the inflectional ending *an* was lost
   clepud 367—regular development from OE preterit *cliopode*
   firiste 462—from OE *fyrest*, without the usual syncope of *e*
   þo 1016—plural article regular development from OE *þā*

ȝougþe 754—retention of *g* from OE *geoguð* after new diphthong had
  formed
fram 107—from OE *fram*
fro 70—from Old Norse *frā*
queynt 294—from OE *cwencan;* eŋct became *eynt* in many dialects
to 416; tweye 584; tweyne 135—all forms in regular use, from OE *twēgen*
  (Masc.), *twā* (Fem. and Neut.)
bileue 926—from OE *gelēaf*
lyue 536—from OE *līf*
  f > *v* in inflected forms between two vowels
hoo 290—OE *hū* > ME *hou; u* sometimes written as *o*
tristed 1051—from Old Norse *treysta*
keste 428—from Old Norse *kasta; a* sometimes became *e* before *s*
cosynus 184—direct from Medieval Latin
abhominacions 206—explained by Sundén (*Göteborgs Högskolas Årskrift,*
  XXXI (1925), p. 7) as due to the "assumed derivation of the word from
  ab homine"
veyne 30—from Old French *vigne;* Fr. *ig* > *ī* or formed a new diphthong
  which generally weakened to *e;* after the weakening the *y* may have
  been added to make a long syllable
3. *Regressive assimilation:*
  osprynge 629—from the regular ME form, *ofspryng;* listed as a variant in
    NED
  þe toþer 1013—*þe oþer* sometimes became *þoþer;* here the scribe kept the
    article as well as a variation of a new form.
4. *Metathesis:*
  þrust 633—from OE *ðyrst, ðurst; þrust* listed in NED as being in use from
    c. 1200 to 1590
  hidre 524—from OE *hider*
  tawth 243—from OE *tāhte*
5. *Loss of consonant:*
  Disappearance of *h* before unaccented vowels and unstressed syllables:
    falsed 314 (falshed)
    eyres 397 (heyres)
    is 217 (his)
  An occasional *w* found instead of the usual *wh:*
    wiche 215
    werwiþ 514
    werfore 995
  Voss of final *d*, a common tendency:
    Godwar 200
    aftirwar 579
  n of *oon* dropped before words beginning with consonant:
    o 77
    oo 779
  Disappearance of ȝ in such words as *nouȝt* in 15th century and occasion-
    ally in the 14th:
    owt 358 (for *auȝt*)
    bout 846 (for *bouȝt*)
6. *Inverse spelling:*
  owȝt 739—from the regular ME form *owt* by analogy with such words as
    nouȝt
  whiȝt 424—from ME form *wiȝt* by analogy with such words as *why; h* of
    wh no longer pronounced in late fourteenth century
  plytes 744—from O.Fr. *pleit;* O.Fr. *ei* > ME *ei* or *e; y* here possibly de-
    veloped with analogy with ME *ei* from OE *eh;* OE *eh* > ME *ei* or *ȳ,*
    e.g. *heigh* or *hy*
  gryntyng 173—from OE *grindan;* possible analogy with pret. and past
    participle where *d* > *t* sometimes after nasal, e.g. *sende* and *sente*
  plete 57—usual form plede (361) also found; possible analogy with words
    where *d* was unvoiced to *t* in final unaccented syllables, especially in
    West Midland dialects; *plete* found in Chaucer, *Troilus* II, 1468

7. *Analogy:*
   axkid 393—possibly a telescoping of the two ME forms, *ask* and *ax*
8. *Weakening of vowel in unstressed syllable or word:*
   a. Medial omission:
      prophte 629
      benfitis 1057
   b. Loss of final *e* in unstressed form:
      pouert 353, 1003
   c. *e* sometimes written *i:*
      hennis 154
      ellis 55
      tixte 882
      forfiteþ 731
   d. *el* written as *ul:*
      littul 1003
   e. Other vowel changes in unaccented word or syllable:
      naþeles 811; neþeles 819
      dalay 756
      os 16 (for *as*)
9. *Shortening or lengthening of vowel:*
   wham 607—early shortening from OE *hwam*
   loost 568—from OE *lust; u* would have lengthened to *o* in the open syllable of the inflected form
10. *Scribal error:*
    a. Plural form where singular is intended:
       maneres 5
       heritages 276
       whiches 516
    b. Letter or syllable incorrectly added:
       regyned 326
       wittenesse 486
       ferendis 2
       beterer 1025
       party 902 (for *part*)
       clepliþ 25
       preciouns 562, 706
       þryþes 654
       Loth 471
       swelwynge 1043
    c. Loss of consonant:
       noubre 885, 979
       comyge 868
       ensauple 685
       openyge 945
       shoden 52
       ouergoo 35

Chapter V

ANALYSIS OF SERMON

A. DATE, AUTHOR, AND PLACE OF DELIVERY

Although problems of date, authorship, and place of delivery of Wimbledon's sermon cannot be absolutely solved, a great deal can be learned from both internal and external evidence. External evidence consists of annotations on the manuscripts concerning date, author, and place of delivery; the sermon itself affords evidence as to date. These two sources of information lead me to consider 1387, 1388, or 1389 the date of delivery; 1387, the date of composition; Thomas Wimbledon, the author; and Paul's Cross, London, the original place of delivery.

Internal evidence is found in all versions of the text except in *T*, *Hr*, *Ul*, from which several pages of the text are omitted. Seven of the manuscripts give no external evidence, namely *C*, *Rb*, *A*, *Hu*, *U*, *H2*, *Ul*. There are nine manuscripts which have external evidence, either early (*Ra*, *H9*, *Hr*) or late (*Ht*, *G*, *Wells*, *S*), or both (*T*, *P*).

Six manuscripts (*Ht*, *G*, *Wells*, *P*, *S*, *T*) have scribblings in the margin added many years after the copying of the text; for this reason they are of doubtful value in determining date, authorship, and place of delivery. A possibility is that the scribblings were copied by the owner of the manuscript from titles given in early printed editions.[1] The six scribblings, which are in late hands, follow:

> *Ht:* Wimbledons Sermon, Camden (p. 1, top margin)
>   *G:* Author R. Wimbledon, Exeat Anglice (p. 201, scribbled in space between preceding treatise and sermon)
> *Wells:* Robertus Wimbleton authore qui floruit tempore Henrici 4 (f.1)[2]
>   *P:* R. Wimbledon his Sermon at Pauls Crosse 1388 in the Raigne of Henry the 4 (f. 65ᵇ)
>   *S:* A Sermon no laser godlie then learned preached at Paules crosse, on the Sondayes Quinquagesima, Anno Mccclxxxix by R. Wymbelion (f. 167ᵛ, page opposite the first page of the sermon)
>   *T:* A sermon preach'd at Paul's Cross, A.D. 1389, by Tho. Wymbleton on Quinquagesima Sunday (p. 242, left margin)

The rubric in *Ra*, though in a different hand from that of the text, appears to have been written about the same time as the text proper by one

[1] See "Chapter II: Descriptions of Manuscripts and Prints. B. The Prints," p. 22.

[2] Wells, *Manual*, Second Supplement, p. 1057.

whose scribal training was similar to that of the scribe of the text; for
this reason more weight should be attached to the information given in
this rubric than to that found in the preceding scribblings. The *Ra* rubric
or incipit reads:

> This sermoun suynge was prechid atte Poulis crosse at two tymes of maistrer
> Thomas Wymbilton in the ȝeer of oure lord a þousand þree hundrid foure score
> and eiȝte (f. 184ᵇ)

The remaining four manuscripts, *T, Hr, H9, P,* which contain rubrics
written by the scribes of the texts, are related.[3] It is probable that an
ur-text of this group contained the information which is given in the
rubrics of these texts. The four rubrics—the first two being incipits; the
last two explicits—follow:

> *H9,* dated by catalogue as "1400" (p. 61):
>
> > þis sermoun folwynge was seid at Poulis in London þe ȝeer of oure lorde
> > 1389 (f. 17ʳ, incipit)
>
> *Hr:*
>
> > Sermo Magistri Thome Wymyldōn, apud Crucem in cimiterio Sancto
> > Pauli London (f. 140ʳ, incipit)
>
> *T,* dated by catalogue "cent. xiv, xv" (p. 273):
>
> > Thomas Wymyldon istum composuit sermonem ad crucem S. Pauli
> > londoun, qui obiit in die omnium sanctorum. amen. Ricardi tercii, con-
> > (qu)estum xv. cuius anime propicietur deus. Amen. (f. 273ᵛ, explicit)
>
> *P,* dated by catalogue "cent. xv (not late)" (p. 72):
>
> > Sermo Thome Wymbeldone london predicatur ad crucem in cimiterio
> > eccl. S. Pauli (f. 73ᵇ, explicit)

Concerning the date, there is both external and internal evidence. The
external evidence, appearing in the scribblings and rubrics just discussed, is concerned with the date of delivery; the internal evidence may
give both the date of composition and the date of delivery. First the external evidence will be examined.

The scribblings and rubrics do not agree as to date of delivery. The
late scribblings, giving the date 1388 (*P*) and Quinquagesima Sunday,
1389 (*S* and *T* late hand), have very little weight in determining the date.
Of more value is *Ra,* which has an earlier rubric, though not in the same
hand as the text; 1388 is the date given by *Ra.* The most significant
manuscript which gives the date is *H9,* whose incipit is in the same hand
as the text; the incipit of *H9* reads 1389. The sermon could have been
preached in 1388 and again in 1389; however, 1389 is the more probable
date of delivery, as the incipit of *H9* is the only one of the early rubrics
which gives the date.

The external and internal evidence do not agree; the internal evidence
indicates a date earlier than 1389. The sermon reads:

[3]See "Chapter III: Relationship of Manuscripts. A. English Manuscripts,"
p. 27.

So it semeþ to þis clerk, þat þe grete Antecrist schulde come in þe fourtenþe hundred ʒeer fro þe birþe of Crist, þe whiche noumbre of ʒeeris is now fulfillid not fully twelue ʒeer and an half lackynge (895-898).

Thus, 1387, the earliest date, may be the date of composition. It is possible that the sermon was preached in that year as well as later in both 1388 and 1389.

From the evidence given by the rubrics above, I consider Thomas Wimbledon to be the author. Here again, the late scribblings are of little value; five of these give the following variations of the author's name:

> Wimbledon—*Ht*
> R. Wimbedon—*G, P*
> R. Wymbelion—*S*
> Tho. Wymbleton—*T*

The *Ra* reading, "Thomas Wymbiltōn," being earlier, is of more value. In the manuscripts which have inscriptions written nearest the time of the sermon, the following forms of the name are given:

> Thome Wymyldōn—*Hr*
> Thomas Wymȳldōn—*T*, explicit
> Thome Wymbeldone—*P*

As *T-Hr-P* are of one family, their readings are considered as one piece of evidence. Even so, the earliest readings agree; and their designation, Thomas Wymbledon, is the most authoritative.

About this Thomas Wimbledon nothing is authentically known. The explicit in *T* states that he died on All Saints' Day, but I find no further information about his death. Owst notes that a certain Thomas Wymbeldone, chaplain to Sir John Sandes, was granted a preaching license in the year 1385 by William of Wykeham;[4] *Wykeham's Register* reads:

> Preacher's license granted to ds. Thomas Wymbeldone, chaplain to sir John Sandes, kt.
> Willelmus, . . . ad exercendum predicacionis officium, et proponendum verbum Dei in ecclesiis quibuscumque nostre diocesis, temporibus ad hoc congruis et consuetis, horis illis, in quibus ecclesiarum rectores et vicarii, ad quorum ecclesias to ex causa premissa contigerit declinare, predicare voluerint, dumtaxat exceptis, licenciam tibi concedimus tenore presencium specialem: inhibentes tamen tibi expresse, ne aliquas conclusiones hereticas seu erroneas, que statum nostre ecclesie Wyntoniensis et tranquillitatem nostrorum subditorum subvertere poterunt asseras seu predices, publice vel occulte, prout ad hoc astringeris ex debito juramenti quovismodo; presentibus per unum annum dum taxat duraturis—Southwark, 28 April 1385.[5]

Such a license would permit the preacher to preach without interference in the parishes visited by him; he was, of course, prohibited from preach-

[4]Owst, *Preaching in Med. England*, p. 360.

[5]*Wykeham's Register*, ed. T. F. Kirby, Hampshire Record Society (London, 1899), Vol. II.

ing any heretical doctrine. A tempting supposition is that this chaplain to Sir John Sandes is the Thomas Wimbledon of "Redde rationem."

Sundén in the preface to his edition of the Hatton manuscript quotes a statement from Benthem's *Engeländischer Kirch-und Schulen-Staat:* " 'Robert Wimbledon ein fürtrefflicher Prediger wie noch zu sehen ist aus seiner Sermon, die er gebalten (*sic*) über diesen Text: Redde rationem villicationis tuae.' "[6] However, as Sundén says, this reference gives no new information concerning Wimbledon.

From his name, Wimbledon, one can conjecture that he was born within the vicinity of London, but there is no fact to verify this supposition. That the sermon was preached at Paul's Cross in London, as both early and late evidence indicate, is no proof that the preacher was a Londoner. Preachers from all England delivered sermons in this famous pulpit—and all kinds of preachers at that, as Owst states, from John Ball to the Archbishop of Canterbury.[7] Bishop Brunton urged all bishops to preach at Paul's Cross:

> At London, because it is the principal city of England, and in that place there is a greater devotion and a more intelligent people, and therefore, it is to be presumed, greater fruit. Moreover, because each bishop of England has subjects or parishioners in London, therefore, when he gives instruction there, it is as though he were preaching to his own people and to the other churches of England in addition, so that in effect, by so doing, each of us may apply to himself that word of the Apostle (2 Cor. xi. 28)—'*that which cometh upon me daily, the care of all the churches*'—of England.[8]

The renown and importance of preaching at Paul's Cross is evidenced in an account, by Stow, of preaching here during holy week, though the grandeur of the occasion would be somewhat diminished on Quinquagesima Sunday. Stow writes:

> And here is to be noted, that time out of minde, it hath beene a laudable custome, that on good Friday in the after noone, some especiall learned man, by appoyntment of the Prelats, hath preached a Sermon at *Paules* crosse, treating of Christs passion: and vpon the three next Easter Holydayes, Monday, Tuesday, and Wednesday, the like learned men, by the like appoyntment, haue vsed to preach on the forenoones at the sayde Spittle, to perswade the Article of Christs resurrection: and then on low Sunday, one other learned man at *Paules* Crosse, to make rehearsall of those foure former Sermons, either commending or reprouing them, as to him by iudgement of the learned Diuines was thought conuenient. And that done, he was to make a sermon of his owne studie, which in all were fiue sermons in one. At these sermons so seuerally preached, the Maior, with his brethren the Aldermen were accustomed to bee present in their Violets at *Paules* on good Fryday, and in their Scarlets at the Spittle in the holidayes, except

[6]Sundén, Preface, "A Famous Middle English Sermon," *Göteborgs Högskolas Årskrift, XXXI* (1925), p. xii.

[7]Owst, *Preaching in Med. England*, pp. 208-209.

[8]Quoted from MS. Harl. 3760, fol. 60ᵛ, and translated by Owst, *Ibid.*, p. 208.

Wednesday in violet, and the Maior with his brethren, on low Sonday in scarlet, at *Paules* Crosse, continued vntill this day.[9]

At the time of Wimbledon's sermon, the pulpit was about one hundred and fifty years old, although it was probably not used for preaching until 1330. Owst gives 1341 as the date of the earliest documentary reference;[10] however, Maclure notes a documentary reference to its use in 1241.[11] The structure was damaged by an earthquake in 1382 and had been repaired for use in 1387, just before Wimbledon's address.[12] The wooden structure built c. 1460 by Bishop Kempe to replace the original cross perhaps reflected the general features of the earlier pulpit. Bishop Kempe's pulpit is described by Stow:

> About the middest of this Churchyeard (of St. Paul's Cathedral) is a Pulpit Crosse of timber, mounted vpon steppes of stone, and couered with leade, in which are sermons preached by learned Diuines euery Sundaye in the forenoone.[13]

Perhaps from a similar structure, in 1387, 1388, or 1389 Thomas Wimbledon preached his sermon, written in 1387.

B. CONTENT

1. *Organization of Medieval Sermons*

Wimbledon's sermon can be best understood when viewed against the background of medieval sermons, and particularly in relation to the type to which it belongs—namely the textual sermon.

Sermons in the fourteenth century can generally be grouped into two types: the ancient or homiletical, and the modern or textual.[1] The homiletical type had little organization; it was a rather informal discourse, described by Henry of Hesse as "the mystical exposition of most of the

[9]John Stow, *A Survey of London*, ed. C. L. Kingsford (Oxford, 1908), I, 167-168.

[10]Owst, *Preaching in Medieval England*, pp. 198-199.

[11]Miller Maclure, *The Paul's Cross Sermons, 1534–1642* (Toronto, 1958), p. 5.

[12]See "Indulgence granted for the Repair of Paul's Cross by William Courtney, Archbishop of Canterbury. 1387." *Documents Illustrating the History of Saint Paul's Cathedral*, edited by W. Sparrow Simpson (Camden Society, 1880), p. 7.

[13]Stow, I, 331.

[1]Harry Caplan, " 'Henry of Hesse' on the Art of Preaching," *PMLA*, XLVIII (1933), p. 341.

Woodburn O. Ross, "Introduction," *Middle English Sermons*, EETS, no. 209 (London, 1940), p. xliii.

terms of a text that aim at a single interpretation."[2] There was no formal introduction or division. Such were the homilies, for example, of Origen (third century), Gregory (sixth century), and Bede (eighth century).

The textual or modern sermon followed a systematic method of analytical organization;[3] this type was used by Albertus Magnus (twelfth century), Thomas Aquinas (thirteenth century), Bonaventure (thirteenth century), and their followers.[4] Tracts on rhetoric and preaching, explaining in detail the modern sermon, appeared in great numbers, and copies were in demand.[5] Caplan tells of John of Ockham's lending his friends, Peter de Vineis and Thomas of Capua, his copy of *Artes dictaminis* at the rate of one goose per week.[6] There was, of course, some opposition to this emphasis on rhetoric; in the ninth century Paulus Albarus wrote:

> The rhetoricians, wordy and redundant, have filled the air with empty wind. The dialecticians, bound fast by rules and entangled on all sides by syllogisms, empty and cunning, are deceitfull spinners of words rather than builders of the art of speech.[7]

However, the opponents were far outnumbered by the advocates of the rhetorical sermons, who included Augustine, Robert of Melun, and John of Salisbury.[8] Rabanus in his *De clericorum instructione* wrote:

> Rhetoric, by which I understand the art of speaking well in civil questions, which seems to belong to mundane science, still is not extraneous to ecclesiastic trial discipline, for skill in this art is useful to the preachers for fluent and proper teaching, as well as for apt and elegant writing, and for delivering a sermon. He does well who learns it fully, and so fits himself to preach God's word.[9]

An anonymous writer of a tract on the art of preaching states that not only learning but also art and method are required for good preaching, "the art of arts, and the science of sciences; . . . for it is the way of life, the ladder of the virtues, and the door of Paradise."[10]

[2]"Tractatulus Eximii Doctoris Henrici de Hassia De Arte Praedicandi Valde Utilis," trans. by Harry Caplan, *PMLA*, XLVIII (1933), p. 348. Hereafter referred to as Henry's Tract.

[3]Harry Caplan, "A Late Medieval Tractate on Preaching," *Studies in Rhetoric and Public Speaking in Honor of James Albert Winans* (New York, 1925), p. 63.

[4]*Ibid.*, pp. 63-64.

[5]See list in Harry Caplan, *Medieval 'Artes Praedicandi,'* Cornell Studies in Classical Philology, XXIV-XXV (1934, 1936).

[6]Harry Caplan, "Classical Rhetoric and Medieval Theory of Preaching," *Classical Philology*, XXVIII (1933), pp. 79-80.

[7]Quoted and translated by Caplan, *Ibid.*, pp. 80-81.

[8]Caplan, "Class. Rhet. and Med. Theory of Preaching," pp. 81-82.

[9]Quoted and translated by Caplan, *Ibid.*

[10]"Tractatulus solemnis de arte et vero modo predicandi," trans. Harry

According to Ross, the modern or textual sermon, extremely popular with the University people, was not generally used in vernacular sermons.[11] However, Wimbledon's English sermon, as well as several vernacular sermons in Ross's collection, is of this type. I shall here outline briefly the organization of the textual sermon.[12]

There are five parts of the textual sermon: 1. Theme, 2. Protheme, 3. Introduction of Theme, 4. Division, and 5. Subdivision; occasionally the Introduction of Theme is incorporated in the Division.

1. THEME. The Theme was usually a verse from the Vulgate Bible.[13] The Aquinas tract stipulates (p. 74) that the Theme should have "a clearly perceived meaning—not incongruous," that it should not be too long or too short, and that it should be filled with homiletical terms.

2. PROTHEME: The Protheme originally existed for the purpose of introducing a prayer.[14] "The Protheme," says Henry of Hesse (p. 349), "is the prelocution designed for the proof of the homiletical terms found in the theme. It should be composed of authorities, drawn from the Bible and from theologians, together with the introduction of authority from philosophy."[15] Occasionally this brief discussion introduced a new topic in some way connected with the Theme.[16] Gradually the Protheme was understood to be anything written between the Theme and its Divisions; however, its function remained the clarification of the truth and importance of the Theme.[17]

3. INTRODUCTION OF THEME: The Introduction of the Theme is discussed only by Thomas Waley; the Aquinas Tract and Henry's Tract lose sight of this section. The reason for the Introduction, as stated by Waley (p. 356), is to catch the attention of the audience, to re-

---

Caplan, *Studies in Rhetoric and Public Speaking* . . . , pp. 70-90. Hereafter referred to as The Aquinas Tract.

[11]Ross, p. xxxii.

[12]I have consulted the following medieval treatises:

Thomas Waley, *De Modo Componendi Sermones Cum Documentis*, ed. Th. M. Charland, *Artes Praedicandi* (Paris, 1936), pp. 325-403.

The Aquinas Tract.

Henry's Tract.

[13]Waley, pp. 341-342.

[14]Th. M. Charland, *Artes Praedicandi* (Paris, 1936), p. 126.

Waley, p. 350.

Homer G. Pfander, *The Popular Sermon of the Medieval Friar in England*, Doctoral dissertation at New York University (New York, 1937), p. 17.

[15]See also The Aquinas Tract, p. 74. Pfander, p. 17.

[16]Waley, p. 350.

[17]Henry's Tract, p. 353.

state the Theme, and to make clear the preacher's intention. Sometimes the Introduction is merely a brief statement of the Theme; at other times it is enlarged by narrative or exposition.[18]

4. DIVISION: The Division, or Process as it was sometimes called, is the separation of the Theme into Principals, usually three, although four are sometimes found.[19] Pfander (p. 17) quotes Etienne Gilson, 'La Technique du Sermon Médiéval,' in a discussion of the Division: "La division doit être approprié, pour instruire; la distinction doit être courte, afin de plaire, ou tout au moins de ne pas ennuyer; le dévelopement doit être utile et efficace, afin de toucher."

5. SUBDIVISION: The Subdivision is a further partioning of the Principals of the Division.[20] In this section of the sermon the Principals are subdivided into Parts or Socii.[21] The number of Parts for each Principal varies; sometimes each of the three Principals is subdivided identically; again, each Principal has its own peculiar Parts.

AMPLIFICATION. After the Division and the Subdivision have been stated, each Principal is developed through the amplification of each of its Parts. There were many means of amplification of which the Aquinas Tract lists nine (p. 76):

> The amplification of sermons is to be accomplished in nine ways: first, through agreements of authorities; second, through discussion of words; third, through the properties of things; fourth, through a manifold exposition or a variety of senses; fifth, through similes and natural truths; sixth, through marking of the opposite, to wit, correction; seventh, through multiplication of synonyms.

Pfander lists others (p. 18): Bible stories, saint's lives, cause and effect, eulogy, and exhortation. Caplan gives also anecdotes and etymology.[22]

CONCLUSION: The sermon generally concludes with a restatement of the theme or a short recapitulation of the sermon,[23] and with a Benediction.[24]

2. *Wimbledon's Sermon*

Part I:

THEME: The Theme is: "Redde rationem villicacionis tue." Lucam xvi. 2. (1) This verse is part of the gospel reading for Wednesday after the first Sunday after Trinity. Possibly the sermon was also preached

---

[18]Waley, pp. 357-359.
[19]Pfander, p. 17. The Aquinas Tract, p. 75. Henry's Tract, p. 352.
[20]Henry's Tract, pp. 352-353. The Aquinas Tract, p. 76.
[21]Pfander, p. 17.
[22]Caplan, "Clas. Rhet. and Med. Theory of Preaching," pp. 88-90.
[23]The Aquinas Tract, p. 90.
[24]Pfander, p. 18.

near or on that day. However the text is a fitting one for Quinquagesima Sunday, the day specified by the scribblings of *S* and *T*.

John Mirk relates Quinquagesima Sunday to the fiftieth year in Jewish law, when all men were freed from bondage, and also to the Day of Doom, when bonds of sin are to be loosened:

> Wherfor þys nowmbur beggynnyþ þyis day, and endyth yn Easter Day schewynge þat yche godys seruants þat ys oppressyd wyþ tribulacyon and takyþ hit meekly yn hert, he schall be made fre yn his resurrecyon: þat ys yn þe day of dome, and be made the ayre of þe kyndome of Heuene.[25]

Speculum Sacerdotale specifies that the term itself

> betokeneþ tyme of remission and foryevenes of penaunce, in the whiche are foryeven alle thynges . . . by penaunce are forgeven the dettes of synne, and men delyuered fro the bondage and servitude of the devel and are turned vnto the possession of here dwellynge place of heuene. This is tyme of fastynge þat we may deserven foryevenes of oure synnes.[26]

Thus, "Redde rationem villicacionis tue," with its emphasis on repentance, forgiveness of sins, and retribution at the day of judgment, is a suitable text for Quinquagesima Sunday.[27]

PROTHEME: The Protheme first literally recounts the parable of the vineyard, Matt. xx. 1-10. (2-12) It then gives an allegorical interpretation (13-56): the householder is Christ; the hours of the day are the ages of the world and the ages of man; the laborers are the three estates of men, prestes, knights, and laborers, each needful to the other. Finally, connecting the parable to the theme, the author points out (82-97) that as each officer or estate labors here so shall he be rewarded "whanne þe day of his rekenyng comeþ þat is þe ende of þis lif"; he urges each man to labor in that estate to which God has called him, and gives Biblical authority for this exhortation (98-118).

INTRODUCTION OF THEME: The Introduction of Theme restates the Theme: "ʒelde rekenynge of þy bailie." (120) This restatement of the Theme is followed by an allusion to the parable of the unjust steward, Lucam xvi. 1-2. (121-126) The author then states his intention: "for now I shal shewe ʒow how ʒe shal dispose ʒou to auoide þanne þe vengeaunce of God, whanne þer shal be tyme of so streyt dome." (131-133)

DIVISION: The division consists of three Principals, three classes of bailiffs: priests, knights, and all other Christian men. In the last group, each man has only to answer for himself; but each man in the first two

[25]*Mirk's Festial*, ed. Theodore Erbe, EETS, ES, no. 96 (London, 1905), p. 74.

[26]Ed. Edward H. Weatherly, EETS, no. 200 (London, 1936), p. 52.

[27]The Gospel reading for Quinquagesima Sunday is Lucam xviii. 31-43; the epistle, I Corinthinos xiii.

groups must account for his treatment of other men as well as for his own conduct. (137-144)

SUBDIVISION: The subdivision specifies that each bailiff must answer three questions: "How hast þou entred?" "How hast þou reulid?" and "How hast þou lyuyd?" (145-150)

AMPLIFICATION: Each question is discussed in relation to each of the three estates. Several means of amplification are used. A favorite type of development is exposition through questions or discussion of a word, e.g. (163-166), "Who brouʒte þe into þis offys? Trewþ oþer symonie? God or þe deuyl? Grace or monye? þe flesh or þe spirit?" On almost every page Biblical and theological authorities are quoted (see below under Author's Reading). Amplification is also accomplished "through marking of the opposite, to wit, correction."[28] For example, consider the statements concerning corruption in the church:

> And ʒif we taken hede trewly what abhominacions ben scaterrid in þe chirche nowadayes among prestis, we shulde well wite þat þey alle comeþ nouʒt into þe folde of Crist by Cristis clepynge for to profite but by oþer weyes to gete hym worldly welþe. . . . In what plente is pride, enuye, wraþe, and coueytise! Whanne were þey so grete as þey beþ now, and so of alle oþer synnes! (206-221)

Similes and natural truths are often used; the following are examples:

> For þey beþ blynde to see how þey shulle go to heuene, but to wynnyng of worldly þyng þey seeþ many weies lik to owles and nytcrowes þat seen betre be nyʒt þan by day. (442-445)

> [Thou art] As Judas was among þe apostelis, as Symound Magus was amonge disciplis, as a candel newe queynt þat stynkeþ al þe hous in stede of a lyʒt lanterne, and as a smoke þat blendeþ mennys eiʒen in place of a clier fier, ʒif þou contrarie þus þe forme of lyuynge þat Crist and his apostelis leften to prestis. (293-298)

Comparison is also used for amplification:

> þerfore it is writen þat 'þe hardest dom shal fallen vpon suche;' an hard dom for þey haueþ mysentrid, an hardere dom for þey haueþ mysreulid, and þe hardeste dom for þey haueþ so cursidly lyued. (303-306)

Development "through a manifold exposition or a variety of senses"[2] is found quite often, though usually only one or two levels of meaning are employed; see, for example, the interpretation above under the protheme and the exposition of the passage from Zechariah. (419-476) Multiplication of synonyms expands the sermon, e.g. (407-409), "And here bewar, ʒee þat haueþ geten any worldly good, oþer take by extorciones, by raueyne, by vsure, oþer by disceit."

[28]The Aquinas Tract, p. 76.
[29]*Ibid.*

Part II:[30]

The second part of the sermon proceeds immediately with a new division and subdivision; there is no formal Introduction.

DIVISION: The Division contains three Principals: "First who shal clepe vs to þis rekenyng, aftirwar, byfore what iuge we shulleþ rekene, and last what punyschynge shal be do to hem þat ben fonden false seruantis and wickid and what reward schal be ȝeue to hem þat ben founden goode and trewe." (579-583)

SUBDIVISION: The Subdivision specifies Parts for only the first of the three Principals. The first question, "Who shal clepe vs to þis rekenyng," is divided into two Parts: one concerned with the day of death, and the other with the day of the general resurrection. (584-592) In turn each of these days is discussed with regard to the three summoners: sickness, age, and death. (593-601) The two last parts of the division are discussed only briefly, and are not divided into Partitions. There is only one judge before whom one can appear, and that is Christ (994-1026); the punishments and rewards consist of woe to the damned and joy to the saved. (1027-1090)

AMPLIFICATION: The development of the Divisions and Subdivisions is much the same as that in Part I. As the organization is a bit more complicated and uneven in this second part, the balance and symmetry are rather distorted. However, the same methods of development are employed in both parts.

CONCLUSION: The sermon ends with a short lyric and a paean of joy:

> Þe ioye of oure herte is ago;
> Oure wele is turned into woo;
> Þe coroune of oure heued is falle vs fro;
> Alas for synne þat we haue doo.

But ioye and ioye and ioye to hem þat beþ saued; ioye in God, ioye in hemself, ioye in oþre þat beþ saued. Also ioye for her trauayle is brouȝt to so gracious an ende; ioye for þey beþ scaped peyne of helle; ioye for þe endeless blisse þat þey haue in syȝt of God.

Cui sit honor et gloria in secula seculorum. Amen. (1093-1102)

C. AUTHOR'S READING

It is likely that the writer of this sermon used one or more of the manuals assembled for preachers of the fourteenth century. These compendia or encyclopaediae of theological knowledge were filled with quotations, arranged under various subjects. Wimbledon did not use

---

[30]The sermon is rather unusual in being divided into two parts; it is the only one thus divided which I have found.

Peter Lombard's *Sententiae*, an especially popular manual, or John Bromyard's *Summa Praedicantium*. However, although I have been unable to trace Wimbledon's quotations to a specific manual, it is probable that he used one. It is also possible that he could have supplied some quotations from his own reading.

For the quotations which I have located, I find that the Vulgate Bible is the book most often used. There are seventy-three Biblical quotations, forty in the Old Testament and thirty-four in the New; these are distributed among thirty-two books of the Bible. Of the Church Fathers, Augustine, Ambrose, Bernard, and Chrysostom are cited. Also I find quotations from the Post-Patristic writers, Gregory I and Isidore of Seville; and from the later theological writers, Innocent IV, Richard of St. Victor, and Hildegarde. From philosophic and scientific writers, Avicenna, Aristotle, and Bartholomew are quoted. I have located six quotations from Gregory, four from Augustine, two from Bartholomew, and only one from each of the rest. The Gloss referred to in several places I have been unable to identify. It is not the *Glossa Ordinaria*, erroneously ascribed to Walafrid Strabo, or Peter Lombard's *Magna Glossatura*, or the Interlinear Gloss by Anselm of Laon.

The passages are variously used. Some are quoted to express the topic under consideration. For example (98-100), " 'euery man see to what astaat God haþ clepid hym and dwelle he þer inne' by trauayle acordyng to his degre" is the topic sentence of the paragraph. The author did not hesitate to quote long passages in order to present an idea. From an Augustinian sermon he quotes a whole paragraph on the greed of covetous men (477-489); another long section, exclaiming against the selfishness of rich men, is from Ambrose's *De Nabuthae*. (516-537)

Elsewhere quotations strengthen or enlarge a proposition; the argument of the topic above from Corinthians is advanced by eight Biblical quotations which, with the topic sentence, constitute the entire paragraph. However, such quotations are usually less concentrated, one quotation often being given in the proof of a statement. For example (248-257), a quotation from one of St. Bernard's sermons merely restates the idea being discussed.

Quotations are employed as examples: Rehoboam exemplifies the tyrant (328-341), and Tobit, the good man under persecution (669-686). The quotation from Innocent, *De Contemptu Mundi*, is composed of examples of persons harmed by covetousness—Baalam, Achor, Judas, etc. (492-503)

Elsewhere the author explains a point by exegesis of a Biblical passage; the vengeance which results from covetousness is shown through explication of a passage from Zechariah (419-476); the approach of the end of the world is proved by the interpretation of the opening of the seven seals in the Apocalypse of Saint John, vi.

Thus, the sermon is amply supplied with quotations from all manner of authorities. Whether the author gathered the material from his own reading or from a manual, his discriminating and varied application of the references shows that he was well in command of the ideas.

Chapter VI

EDITORIAL PRINCIPLES

This text, a reconstructed common original of all the manuscripts, is both a diplomatic text and a critical text. The text itself is established by a critical analysis of the English texts, with the majority reading generally determining each reading of the reconstructed text.

The text is based on Corpus Christi (*C*), the manuscript which collation proves to be closest to the reconstructed common original.[1] The changes made in *C* are indicated at the bottom of each page in the top set of variants (entitled "*C*"); by combining these with the text, the reader will obtain a diplomatic text of *C*.

The important variants in the other English manuscripts are printed below the variants of *C*, under "*Var.*" When the two sets of variants, forming the critical apparatus, are combined with the text, the reader is provided with a critical text of the sermon. The major differences of word and phrase are noted, as are omissions; but differences in spelling, word order, and minor words are not indicated.

In spelling and general form the reconstructed text follows *C*. The punctuation and capitals in the basic text are editorial; the punctuation is added to make the text more readable; first words and proper names are capitalized. Quoted passages which I have located are placed within quotation marks; omissions within the quotation are not noted.

The capitals, punctuation, and paragraph marks of the manuscript are not transcribed. For some capitals the manuscript has only a blank space in the text with a small letter in the margin for the illuminator. I have inserted these letters in the text with no annotation.

The word divisions in *C* are not observed; wrongly divided words are printed as one, e.g. sow le: sowle (450), bly*n* de: bly*n*de (442), coue ytise: coueytise (456); two words written as one are separated in the text, e.g. outfirst: out first (6), froþerote: fro þe rote (31), spirit*isin*herewyng*is*: spirit*is* i*n* her*e* wyng*is* (430). Words obviously misspelled but intelligible are not corrected, e.g. clepliþ (25), noubre (885), Godwar (200).

Abbreviations are expanded, and these expansions are indicated by italics. Abbreviations with corresponding expansions are listed below:

[1] See "Chapter III: Relationship of Manuscripts. A. English Manuscripts," p. 27.

⎯	m, n	bar̄thus, B	Bartholomeus
con̄	cion	ier̄lm	Ierusalem
ꝟ	re	B'	Bernardus
...ᛜ	ri	ih̄u	Iesu
...◌	er, ir	ih̄c	Iesus
...◌	ur	jo̅h	Johan
...ᵃ	ra, a, ma	mat̄h	Matheu
ꝼ	per, par	Au⁹	Augustinus
ꝓ	pro	vb	verbis
ꝗ	ser	doⁱ	domini
...c	ec	cᵒ	capitulo
...ꝛ	is	sᵗᵒ	sexto
...⁹	us, is	pᵒ	primo
ħ, ꝉ	he, le, lis	li, l.	liber
9	con	scs	sanctus
ꝯ	cius, cionis	dn̄s	dominus
þᵗ	þat	d̄s	deus
þᵘ	þou	op̄c	omnipotens
wᵗ	wiþ	s̄t	sunt
÷	and	nl̄m	naturalium
qᵉstioun	questioun	pat'n̄r	pater noster
anc̄rist	antecrist		

Abbreviations for books of the Bible, referred to in the margin, have been expanded into the form found in the Vulgate.

The readings of the reconstructed text are established by a critical analysis of the English texts, the two Latin versions being considered whenever any question concerning a reading arises. In most cases the majority reading determines a questionable word; the decision is reached by an actual counting of the *variae lectiones*, one vote being given for the reading of the family *T-Hr-H9-P*, and one for *A-H2*. The following are examples of variant readings:

   79: bakeris
     Rb, S, T-Hr-H9-P, A-H2, U, Hu—bakeris
     Ht, Ra (expunged), C—laboreris
   207: ben
     Ht, Ra, Hr-H9-P, A-H2, U—ben
     S *lh.*—ben
     C, Hu—*om.*
   218: ȝow
     Ht, Ra, H9-Hr-P, A-H2, U, Hu—ȝow
     C, S—*om.*
     T, Rb—*out*

371: ʒelde
 Ht, Rb, S, T-Hr-H9, A-H2, U, Hu—ʒelde
 C, Ra—*om.*
 P—gyue

Whenever a word is omitted from *C*, it is spelled according to the dialect of *C*, which is the London dialect.

There are occasional exceptions to the rule of the majority count for the determining of a reading, e.g.:

462-463: þe first woman þat is pride haþ tweye wengis
 P, Hu, U—þe firste woman þat is pride haþ two wenges
 Hr *mg.*—þe firste woman þat is pride haþ two wenges
 S—þe first haþ two wenges
 C, Ht, Ra, Rb, T-H9, A-H2—*om*
381: He schal not take gouernayl
 T-Hr-H9-P, A-H2,—he schal not take gouernayl
 C, Ra, S, U, Hu—he shal take gouernayl
 Ht—How shal he take gouernayl

In the first example, the minority reading, "þe firste woman þat is pride haþ two wenges," is chosen for clarity. Obviously from the context the clause is needed to complete the thought. There are two women, each having two wings; the wings of the first are described, then the wings of the second. The additional clause is needed to clarify the explication which follows concerning the first woman.

In the second example, the majority reading, "he shal take gouernayl," is rejected for two reasons. First, from the context, this reading, although that of *C*, is obviously incorrect. Second, the passage is a translation from Gregory's *Moralium:* "Non autem debet hominum ducatum suscipere, que necit homines bene vivendo praeire,"[2] which contains the *not.*

There are a few cases in which the *variae lectiones* of a reading are by count evenly divided. At such times the reading of *C* is chosen for the reconstructed text. Consider the following example:

342: lowere
 Ra, S, C—lowere
 Rb, A-H2, U—leders
 Ht—lord
 T-Hr-H9-P—reuler
 Hu—lawere or ruler

I have chosen *lowere* for the reconstructed text. *Lowere* is possibly a Middle English variant of *lord.* Jordan lists both *loverde* and *loor* as

[2]Gregorius I, "Moralium," Liber xxiv, ch. 25, paragraph 54, Migne, *Paterlogiae Cursus Completus, Series Latina* (Paris, 1882), LXXVI, col. 318.

variants.[3] *D* was sometimes lost after *r*,[4] which partly explains how *lowere* can be a variant of *loverde*. The choice of *lowere* from the other readings is based upon two facts. First, *lowere* is the reading of the three best texts, *C, S, Ra.* Second, it is the less clear reading, and the various scribes, in their attempt to elucidate the text, would probably change the less familiar term to a better known one; thus the variety of readings can be explained. Falconer Madan states that "a difficult or obscure reading is better than one which is, from the point of view of the copyist, fuller and easier."[5]

Following the Collation of Texts, numbered according to the lines of the text, are found my critical notes, presenting references to sources or to parallel passages and data concerning questionable readings.

[3]Richard Jordan, *Handbuch der mittelenglischen Grammatik*, rev. H. Ch. Matthes (Heidelburg, 1934), pp. 133, 180.
[4]*Ibid.*, p. 180.
[5]Falconer Madan, *Books in Manuscript,* 2nd edition (London, 1927), p. 76.

SIGLA AND OTHER ABBREVIATIONS

A	British Museum, Additional 37677
C	Cambridge, Corpus Christi 357
G	Cambridge, Gonville and Caius 334 (Latin)
H2	Helmingham Hall LJ II 2
H9	Helmingham Hall LJ II 9
Hr	British Museum, Harley 2398
Ht	Oxford, Bodleian, Hatton 57
Hu	Huntington Library HM 502
P	Pepys 2125
Ra	British Museum, Royal 18 A xvii
Rb	British Museum, Royal 18 B xxiii
S	Cambridge, Sidney Sussex 74
T	Cambridge, Trinity 322
U	Oxford, University College 97
U1	Cambridge, University Library Ii III 8 (Latin)

r, v recto, verso of a folio

a, b designation of paginal columns: a—column 1, b—column 2

/ beginning of a new page or column in manuscript

* marginal reference

( ) editorial interpolation

Var Variants of all English mss. other than *C*, the variants of which are listed separately

out omission of a long passage

add adds, add, added

om. omits, omit, omitted

mg. margin

lh. late hand

ins. above inserted above

illeg. illegible

Chapter VII

THE TEXT AND VARIANT READINGS

fol 1ʳᵃ "Redde racionem villicacionis tue." Luce sexmo decimo. (2)

My dere ferendis, ʒe shullen vndirstonde þat Crist

*Matthaeum
xxº. (1-10)*

Iesus, auctour and doccour of trewþe, in his book of þe
gospel liknyng þe kyngdom of heuene to an housholdere,
seiþ on þis maneres: "Lik is þe kyngdom of heuene to an   5
housholdynge man þat wente out first on þe morwe to
hire werkemen into his vine. Also aboute þe þridde,
sixte, nyenþe, *and* eleuene houris he wente out *and*
fond men stondynge ydel *and* sey to hem: Go ʒee into
my vyne *and* þat riʒt is I wole ʒeue ʒow. Whanne þe day   10
was ago, he clepid his styward *and* heet to ʒeue eche
man a peny."

*Colossen-
ses primo.
(18)*

To spiritual vndirstondyng þis housholdere is oure
lord Iesu Crist, þat "is heed of þe houshold of holi
chirche." *And* þus he clepiþ men in diuerse houris of þe   15

C

7 Also] o *blotted.*   9 hem] e *blotted.*   11 *and* heet] *blotted.*

Var

1 sexmo decimo] xvi chapitre Ht, Ra, H9, Hu; *om.* T, A, H2.   2 My dere
ferendis] worchippful Rb.   3 Iesus] *om.* S.—trewþe] al truþe Ht, Ra, Hu.
6 housholdynge man] householder Ht, A, H2; housbonde man Ra.—out]
om. Rb.—morwe] *add ins. above lh.* tide H2.   7 vine] vyneʒerde Rb, Hr, T,
U, P, *lh.* H2—þridde] *add* hour P, *lh.* H2.   8 nyenþe] nynþe houre Hu.—*and*
eleuene] *om.* U.   9 ʒee] *om.* P.   10 vyne] vyneʒerde Ht, Rb, S, T, Hr, U, P;
ʒerd *mg. lh.* Hu, H2.—riʒt] *om.* Hu.   11 heet] baad Ra; bad hym Ht, Rb, A,
H2; heet hym Hu.—eche] every P.   12 man] of ys werkemen Rb.   13 To] to
youre Rb; the H2; to þe Hu.—spiritual] gostly P; *add mg.lh.* the calling of
Gods church S.   14 of þe] of al þe T, Hr, P.   15 he] *om.* Ra, Rb, S, H9, A,
Hr, U.

Matthaeum xx   *om.* Ra, T, Hr, U, Hu, P; *illeg.* A.

Colossenses primo] om. Ht, Ra, Rb, T, Hr, U, P.

61

day, þat is in diuerse ages of þe world; os in tyme of
lawe of kynde he clepide by enspirynge Abel, Ennok, Noe,
and Abraham; in tyme of þe olde lawe Moyses, Dauid,
Ysaye, and Jeremie; and in tyme of grace apostelis,
martiris, and confessoures, and virgines. Also he clepeþ   20
men in diuerse agis, summe in childhod as Jon Baptist,
summe on stat of wexenge as Jon þe Euangelist, summe in
stat of manhod as Petir and Andrew, and summe in old age
as Gamaliel and Josep of Aramathie. And alle þese he
clepliþ to trauayle / on his vyne, þat is þe chirche,   25
and þat on diuerse maneres.

    For riȝt as ȝee seeþ þat in tilienge of þe material
vine þere beeþ diuerse laboreris: for summe kuttyn awey
þe voyde braunchis; summe maken forkes and rayles to
beren vp þe veyne; and summe diggen awey þe olde erþe   30
fro þe rote and leyn þere fattere. And alle þeise offices
ben so nescessarie to þe veyne þat ȝif eny of hem fayle
it schal harme gretly or distroye þe vyne. For but ȝif

fol. 1ʳᵇ appears at line 25 left margin.

C
16 þat is in di] *hole in MS.* 25 his vyne] *illeg.* 27 seeþ] s *illeg.* 28 kuttyn]
ut *erased.* 32 so] *ins. above.* 33 harme] *mg.*
Var
16 is] *add ins. above lh.* to say H2.—os] for as Rb; *ins. mg. lh.* seen H2. 17 he
clepide] *om.* Ra.—by] *om.* Hr, T. 19 apostelis] he cald apostles Rb. 21 men]
many men T, Hr, P.—Jon] seyn Johan P. 22 Jon] Seynt Johan P. 24
Gamaliel] Samuel U, Hr.—alle] *om.* T, Hr, P.—he] ben Rb, A, H2. 25 vyne]
vyneȝerd Rb, T, U, P; *add ins. above lh.* yarde H2.—þe chirche] holi chirche
Ht; in his chirche A, H2. 28 laboreris] labores Ht, Ra, Rb, S, Hu. 29 þe
voyde braunchis] þe braunchys þat ben voyde Ht; þe old braunchys Rb, A,
H2; þe braunchis H9. 31 and leyn] forto legge P.-alle] *om.* Ht. 32 eny] on
T, Hr, P. 33 harme gretly or] *om.* T, Hr, P.—or distroye] to Ht.—For] *om.*
Ht, Ra.

þe vine be kut, he schal wexe wilde; but ʒif she be
rayled, she shal be ouergoo wiþ netles *and* wedis; *and*   35
but ʒif þe rote be fettid wiþ donge, she for feblenesse
shold wexe barayne.

    Ryʒt so *in* þe chirche beeþ nedeful þes þre offices:
presthod, knyʒthod, *and* laboreris. To prestis it falliþ
to kutte awey þe voide braunchis of synnis wiþ þe swerd   40
of her*e* tonge. To knyʒt*is* it falliþ to lette wrongis *and*
þeft*is* to be do, *and* to mayntene goddis lawe *and* hem þat
ben techeris þer of, *and* also to kepe þe lond fro enemyes of oþer londes. *And* to laboreris it falleþ to
trauayle bodily *and* wiþ her*e* sore swet geten out of þe   45
erþe bodily liflode for h*em and* for oþer parties. *And*
þese stat*is* beþ also nedeful to þe chirche þat no*n* may
fol. 1ᵛᵃ wel be*n* wiþouten oþer. For ʒif presthod lackede / þe
puple for defaute of knowy*ng* of Goddis lawe shulde wexe

C
34 kut] *erased.* 35 rayled] r *illeg.* 40 synnis] ni *illeg.*
Var
35 rayled] vpprayled Rb.—ouergoo] ouergroun Ht.—netles *and*] *om.* Rb.
36 for feblenesse] *om.* Ht. 39 prestis] presthode T, Hr, P. 41 falliþ] *add* to
kutte awei þe braunchis H9. 41-42 *and* þeftis to be do] *om.* P. 43 ben] *om.*
Ht. 44 of oþer londes] þer of Rb. 46 hem] hemself T, H9, Hr, A, P, H2.—
oþer parties] oþere two parties A, H2; two oþer partyes P. 48 lackede]
wantyd Ht. 49 shulde] we schulde S.

wilde on vices *and* deie gostly. *And* ʒif þe knythod   50
lackid *and* men to reule þe puple by lawe *and* hardnesse,
þeues *and* enemies shoden so encresse þat no man sholde
lyuen in pes. And ʒif þe laboreris weren not, boþe
prestis *and* knyʒtis mosten bicome acremen *and* heerdis,
and ellis þey sholde for defaute of bodily sustenaunce   55
deie.

*vj Natura-
lium,
parte
quinta,
capitulo
primo   *And* herfore seiþ a gret clerk, Auycenne, þat "euery
vnresonable beest, ʒif he haue þat þat kynde haþ ordeyned
for hym as kynde haþ ordeyned it, he is sufficiaunt to
lyue by hymself wiþouten eny oþer of þe same kynde." As   60
ʒif þere were but one hors oþer oon sheep in þe world,
ʒit ʒif he hadde graas *and* corn as kynde haþ ordeyned
for suche bestes, he shulde lyue wel jnow. But ʒif þer
were but oon man in þe world, þouʒ he hadde all þat good
þat is þer in, ʒit for defaute he scholde die, or his   65
lif shulde be worse þan ʒif he were nouʒt. *And* þe cause
is þis: for þyng þat kynde ordeyneþ for a mannis sus-

C
53 þe] *om.*
Var
51 lackid] wantid Ht; *om.* A, H2.—*and* hardnesse] of armes P.   52 þeues]
iews T, Hr, P.—so] *om.* Ht, H9.—no man sholde] men shulden not U.—
sholde] myʒte Hu.   53 pes] rest H2.—laboreris] labores Hr.—weren not]
lakkeden U.   57 Auycenne] *om.* Ht; Innocente Hr; Aunselme Hu.   59 for
hym] *om.* Ht; for suche beestis Hu.—as kynde haþ ordeyned it] *om.* Ht, T,
Hr, P; *deleted* H2.   60 eny] helpe of eny T, Hr, P; eny helpe of H9.   64 þat
good] *om.* Hu.   65 defaute] *add* of knowledge H2.—he sholde die or] *om.* H2.
65-66 or his lif shulde be worse þan ʒif he were nouʒt] *om.* Rb.   66 nouʒt] aut
erased H2; *ins. mg. lh.* a resonbil best H2.
   vj Naturalium, parte *quinta, capitulo primo] om.* Ht, Ra, Rb, H2, T, Hr, A,
U, Hu; Avicenna *mg.* Ht, U.

tinaunce wiþoutyn oþer arayng þan it haþ of kynde acordiþ nouȝt to hym. As þouȝ a man haue corn as it comeþ
fro þe erþe, ȝit it is no mete acordynge to hym into it   70
be by mannis craft chaungid into bred. And þouȝ he haue

fol. 1ᵛᵇ flesche oþer fissche, ȝit while / it is raw, as kynde
ordeyneþ it, forto it be by mannis trauayle soþen,
rosted, oþer bake, it acordiþ not to mannis liflode.
And ryȝt so wolle þat þe sheep beriþ mot by many diuerse   75
craftis *and* trauaylis be chaungid er it be able to cloþe
eny man. *And* certis o man bi hymsilf shulde neuere don
alle þise labouris. *And* þerfore seiþ þis clerk, it is
nede þat summe beþ acremen, summe bakeris, summe makeris
of cloþ, *and* summe marchaundis to fecche þat þat o lond   80
fauteþ from anoþer þer it is plente.
    And certis þis shulde be o cause why euery staat

C
72 while] h *ins. above.* 79 bakeris] laboreris.
Var
67-68 for a mannis sustinaunce wiþoutyn oþer arayng þan it haþ of kynde]
om. Rb. 68 add mg. lh. yit it be odir wyse H2.—haþ of kynde] is of kytt H2;
mg. lh. one kynd H2.—of] *add* his owen P. 69 hym] man sustynauns withowt
oþur arayinge Rb. 70 fro] oute of T, Hr, P.—into] tyll Rb, A, U, H2; fort P.
71 chaungid] turned A, H2. 72 ȝit] *om.* H2, A. 73 ordeyneþ] askiþ Ht.—
forto] ere þat A, H2; tyll Rb; til þat U, P; vnto Ht.—by mannis trauayle] tyl
it be T, Hr; by mans craft and trayueyll Rb; *om.* P. 73-74 soþen, rosted,
oþer bake] *om.* S. 75 ryȝt so] *om.* A; þe H2. 77 neuere] *add* wel P. 79 nede]
nedeful Ht.—summe beþ acremen] sum men ben acremen Ht.—bakeris]
laboreris HT; *marked for expunction* Ra.—summe . . . summe . . . summe . . .]
add men T, Hr. 81 fauteþ] faylyþ T, Hr, P.—anoþer] *add* and so bringe it fro
anoþer lond H9; *add* lond P. 82 o] *om.* H2.

shul loue oþer *and* me*n* of o craft shulde neiþer hate ne
despise me*n* of anoþer craft siþ þey beþ so nedeful euer-
ych to oþer. *And* ofte þilke craftis þat seme*n* most vn-   85
honest my3the*n* worst be forbore. *And* o þyng y dar wel
seye: þat he þat is neiþer traueylynge i*n* þis world on
prayeris *and* prechynge for helpe of þe puple, as it falliþ to prestis; neiþer in fy3tinge a3en*is* tyrau*n*tis *and*
enemyes, as it falliþ to kny3t*is*; neiþer trauaylynge on   90
þe erþe, as it falliþ to laboreris—wha*n*ne þe day of his
rekeny*n*g comeþ þat is þe ende of þis lif, ry3t as he
lyuede her*e* wiþoutyn trauayle, so he shal þer*e* lacke þe
reward of þe peny, þat is þe endeles ioye of heuene. And
as he / was her*e* lyuynge aft*ir* noon staat ne ordre, so   95
he shal be put þa*n*ne "i*n* þat place þat noon ordr*e* is i*n*ne,
but eu*er*elastynge horrou*r*" *and* sorwe þat is i*n* helle.

fol. 2ʳᵃ
*Job xᵒ
capitulo.
(22)

C
95 ordre] *ins. above.*
Var
84 anoþer] *om.* A.   84-85 siþ þey . . . þilke craftis] *om.* T; *mg.* Hr.—euerych]
ech Hu, H9, A, H2.   85 *And*] For H2, P.—ofte] *om.* P; *add ins. above lh.*
tymes H2.—þilke] suche Rb; *add ins. above lh.* tymes H2.   86 *And* o] anoþer
T, P.—þyng] *om.* A.   87 traueylynge] traueylynge here Rb.—world] *add in*
studiynge H9, *mg. lh.* S; *add in* study3nge in Godes lawe P; *add in* stondynge
T.   87-88 on prayeris *and*] ne preieing ne Ht.   88 prechynge] trewe prechyng
T, H9, Hr, P.—helpe] helþe Ht.   88-89 falliþ to prestis; neiþer] *mg. lh.* S.
89 in fy3tinge] ne defendynge Rb; rulynge þe puple mayntenynge ne defendynge H9, *mg. lh.* S; reulinge þe peple maynteynynge hem ne defendyng
fro þefes in fy3tynge T, Hr, P.—a3en*is*] fro H9, S.—tyrau*n*tis *and*] *om.*
H9, S.   90 enemyes] *mg. lh.* S.—trauaylynge] trauailyng in dyuers craftes T,
H9, Hr, P; *add mg. lh.* in diuerse craftes S.   90-91 on þe erþe] *om.* Rb, H9.
91 *add mg. lh.* everyone in his calling Ra.   93 wiþoutyn] *add mg. lh.* labor and
trauayle H2.—lacke] wante Ht; *om.* Rb.   94 endeles ioye of] joy þat is endlis
in T, Hr, P.   96 put þa*n*ne] *om.* Rb.—þa*n*ne] *om.* H9, A, H2.—i*n*ne] *om.* P.
97 horrou*r*] errour Ra, Rb, T, H9, Hr.—i*n* helle] in þe pitt of helle Rb.

     Job . . .] in text T, Hr, P; *om.* U, Hu.

Herfore "euery man see to what astaat God haþ clepid
hym and dwelle he þer inne" by trauayle acordyng to his
degre. Prima Corinthios vijᵒ. (20). þou þat art a la-
borer or a crafti man "do þis trewli." 2 Timotheum 4ᵒ.   100
(5). "ȝif þou art a seruant oþer a bond man be soget and
low" in drede of displesynge "to þy lord." Prima Petri 2ᵒ.
(18). ȝif þou art a marchaunt, "disceyue nouȝt þy broþer"
in chafferynge. Prima Thessalonicenses 4ᵒ. (6). ȝif   105
þou art a knyȝt oþer a lord, "defende þe pore man and nedy
fram his houndis þat willen harmen hym." Psalmo 81. (4)
ȝif þou art a iustise oþer a iuge, "go nouȝt into þe ryȝt
hond" by fauour, "neyþer into þe lefte honde" to punysche
eny man for hate. Proverbia 4ᵒ. (27). ȝif þou art a   110
prest "vndirnyme, praye, and reproue in alle maner pacience

C
100 þat] *om.* 102 a bond] *om.* a. 108 a iuge] *om.* a. 109 þe lefte] *om.* þe.
Var
98 see] see to ys degree Rb. 99 by *trauayle* acordyng to] trewly trauailynge
after P. 100 degre] degree so þat þou be not fon in ydelnes of synne Rb.—
Prima . . . vijᵒ] *om.* U, Hu; *mg.* Ra, S, H9, A, H2, Rb; 2 Corinthios vijᵒ *mg.* Ht.
101 2 Timotheum 4ᵒ] *om.* U, Hu, Ht; *mg.* Ra, S, H9, A, H2; Titum 2 Rb.
103 drede] degre nouȝt T, P, Hr; degree H9, A, H2.—*Prima Petri 2ᵒ*] *om.* Rb,
U, Hu; *mg.* Ra, S, A, H2; 1 Petri 3 *mg.* Ht; Prima Timotheum 3 *mg.* H9.
104 nouȝt] not þe peple ne T, Hr, P. 105 chafferynge] marchaundise A, H2.
—*Prima . . . 4ᵒ*] *om.* Ht, Ra, U, Hu; *mg.* Rb, S, H9, A, H2; *Prima* Thessaloni-
censes xᵐᵒ *in text* Hr, *blurred in text* T. 107 hym] *add* and ever to be redy for
to stond for þe trouth of Goddys lawe Rb.—*Psalmo 81*] *om.* Ht, Ra, Rb, U,
Hu; *mg.* S, T, H9, A, H2. 108 oþer a iuge] *om.* P.—into] owt of Rb.
109 hond . . . honde] syde . . . syde Rb. 109-110 to . . . hate] *om.* Rb; *add*
for hate in hardnes for duresse, but loke þou be free of þi connynge and ȝeff
þe pore man counsell in truth, and namely to wedowes and to moderles
children Rb; *add mg. lh.* or wrath H2. 110 Proverbia 4ᵒ] *om.* Ra, U, Hu;
mg. Rb, S, T, H9, A, H2. 111 maner] *om.* Rb, A, H2.

and doctrine." *Duo* Tim*o*theum 4º. (2). Glo*ss*ario. Vndirnyme
þilke þat beþ n*e*cligent; p*r*aie for þilke þat beþ obedie*n*t;
reproue he*m* þat ben vnobedie*n*t to God. *And* so eu*e*ri ma*n*
trauayle i*n* his degr*e*; for wha*nn*e þe eue*n* is come þat is   115
þe ende of þe world, "þa*nn*e eu*e*ry ma*n* shal take r*e*ward,
good oþ*e*r euyl, aft*ir* þat he haþ trauayled her*e*." *Prima*
Cor*i*n*thios iijº. (8).

My wordes þat y haue take*n* to make*n* of þis s*e*rmou*n*
fol. 2ʳᵇ   beþ þus myche to seye: / "Ȝilde r*e*keny*n*ge of þy bailie."   120
Crist, auctor of pite *and* louer*e* of þe saluaci*o*n of his
peple, i*n* þe p*r*oce*ss*e of þis gospel enformeþ eu*e*riche
ma*n*, þat is his baile, by man*e*r of a parable of a bayly
þat he spekeþ of to araye hy*m* for to answer*e* of þe goodis
þat God haþ bytake*n* hy*m* wha*nn*e þe day of stre*y*t r*e*keny*n*g   125

C
113 for] *om.*—beþ obedie*n*t] be beþ obedie*n*t *with* be *expunged.*   124 for] *om.*
Var
out   117-125 þat he haþ . . . r*e*keny*n*g Hu.
112 *Duo* Tim*o*theum 4º. Glo*ss*ario] *om.* Ra, U, Hu; *mg.* S, H9, A, H2; glossa
mg. T; Duo Timotheum Ht, Rb.   112-114 Vndirnyme . . . God] *om.* Rb.
113 n*e*cligent . . . obedie*n*t] *om.* H9.—þilke] hem T, P, Hr, A, H2.   114 be*n*]
om. Ht.   115 eue*n*] ende H9.   116 take] *add* hes H2.   117 haþ] haþ deserued
and Hr.—her*e*] *add* Redde rationem et cetera H9; *add* in þis lif Redde rationem
villicacionis tue P.   117-118 *Prima* Cor*i*n*thios iijº] *om.* Ht. Ra, U, A, H2; *mg.*
Rb, S, T.   119 to] *add* Redde rationem villicationis et cetera H2.—make*n* of]
speke at þis tyme Rb; *add* þis talkyng of T, Hr.   120 Ȝilde . . . bailie] *mg.* Hr;
Redde racionem villicacionis tue Hr; Redde *plus illeg. words* T.—Ȝilde] *add* þi
S, A, H2.—bailie] bayllyshipp Rb.   121 pite] pors T; pes and of pite P.
124 to araye] byddyng to aray T, Hr, P.

shal come, þat is þe day of doom. *And* so I at þis tyme,
þourȝ þe helpe of God, folwynge hym þat is maister of so
gret auctorite, by þe cause þat y knowe no þyng þat shulde
more drawe awey mannis vnresounable loue fro þe passynge
ioye of þis world þan þe mynde of þat dredful rekenyng,   130
as myche as y suffice for now I shal shewe ȝow how ȝe
shal dispose ȝou to auoide þanne þe vengeaunce of God,
whan þer shal be tyme of so streyt dome þat we shulle
Matthaeum 12. (36) "ȝelde rekenyng of euery ydel word þat we hauen spoken."
For þanne shal it be sayd to vs, *and* we shul not mow   135
flee it: "ȝelde rekenynge of þy baylie."

But for ferþer proces of þis firste partie of þis
Nota de iij villici sermoun, ȝe shal wite þat þer beþ þre bayleis þat shullen
be clepid to þis streyte rekenyng, tweyne to answere for
hemself *and* for oþer, þat beþ prestis þat han cure of   140

C
137 ferþer] oure.
Var
out 126-140 Hu.
127 hym þat is] Crist Rb.   129 drawe] dryue A, H2.   133 of so] *om.* Rb.—
so] *om.* U, A, H2.—dome] *om.* Rb.—þat we shulle] þan euery man Rb.
135 *and*] where Rb.—not] *mg. lh.* H2.—mow] *om.* U, Rb.   137 ferþer] *om.*
Ra, Rb; first U.   138 sermoun] lesson T, Hr, P.—þre] *om.* Ht.   139 clepid]
called Rb.—streyte] *om.* S.—answere] *add* both Rb.
  *Matthaeum 12] *om.* C, Ht, Ra, S, T, H9, Hr, U, H2; illeg. A.
  *Nota . . .] *mg. lh.* C; *om. all other MSS.*

fol. 2ᵛᵃ mennis soulis, *and* temperal lordis / þat hauen gouernayle
of peplis; and þe þridde baylie shal acounte only for
hymself, *and* þat is euerich oþer Cristene man, of þat he
haþ resceyued of God.

   And euerich of þyse shal answere to þre questiouns: 145
þe firste questioun, how hast þou entred; þe secunde, how
hast þou reulid; *and* þe þridde, how hast þou lyuyd. *And*
ȝif þou canst wel assoyle þese þre questiouns, was þer neuere
noon erþely lord þat so rewardiþ his seruaunt wiþoute com-
parisoun as þy Lord God shal reward þe, þat is wiþ lif *and*   150
ioye þat euere shal laste. But on þat oþer side, ȝif þou
wilt now be recheles of þyn owen welfare *and* take noon hede
of þis rekenyng, ȝif þat deþ take þe sodeynly so þat þou
passe hennis in dedly synnes, as þou wost neuere what shal
falle to þe, alle þe tongis þat euere weren oþer shal be   155
mowen not telle þe sorwe *and* woo þat þou shalt suffre.
þerfore þe desire of so gret ioie *and* þe drede of so gret

C
153 þe] *ins. above.*
Var
out 141-153 mennis . . . deþ take Hu.
142 baylie] *om.* Rb, A.—only] *om.* Ht. 143 oþer] *om.* Ht, Rb, T, H9, Hr, A,
H2. 145-147 *add mg. lh.* Amice quomodo Intrasti/ rexisti/ vexisti redde
rationem H2. 149 noon] *om.* Ht; sion Rb.—so] shall Rb. 149-150 wiþoute
comparisoun] like Rb. 150 God] *om.* Rb, T, Hr, P, A.—lif *and*] vnnombrable
Rb. 152 owen] *add* reknynge P.—welfare] helþe Rb. 153 take] com to Rb.
153-154 sodeynly . . . hennis] *om.* Ht. 154 hennis] *om.* Ht; sodenly as is
custom ys and þou take þin endynge Rb. 155 falle] *om.* Hr.—oþer] *add* euere
Rb, T, H9, Hr, P, A, U. 156 shalt] *add* euere be in and H9; *add* be inne and
T, Hr, P.—suffre] *add* withowt ende Rb. 157 gret] þe endeles Rb.

peyne, þouȝ louedrede of God were not *in* þyn herte, sholde
make þe to þenke euermore þat þou shalt ȝeue rekenyng of þy
baylie.   160

Matthaeum 22. (12)

     Þerfore, as I seie, þe first questioun þat shal be
purposid to þe firste baylif, þat is a prelat oþer a curat
of mennis sowlis, is þis: How hast þou entred? "Frend,

fol. 2ᵛᵇ

how entredist þou hidir?" / Who brouȝte þe into þis offys?
Trewþe oþer symonie? God or þe deuyl? Grace or monye?   165
Þe flessh or þe spirit? Ȝif þou þy rekenyng ȝif þou
canst. Ȝif þou canst nouȝt, I rede þat þou tarie nouȝt
to leerne. For vpon hap or nyȝt þou shalt be clepid, *and*
ȝif þanne þou stonde dowmbe for vnkunnyng or ellis for
confusioun of þy conscience, þou falle into þe sentence   170

Var

158 louedrede] loue and þe drede Rb; loue S; oure lord P; *add mg. lh.* ne
drede S.—of God] *om.* H9. 158-159 sholde . . . euermore] ȝitt þou shuldes
fasten þis in þi mynde Rb. 161 þerfore, as I seie] and so Rb.—I] *om.* S; *add
mg. lh.* it S.—*add mg. lh.* a fairoe to sinne for to thinke S.—seie] *add mg. lh.*
to thot S. 162 *add mg. lh.* the first bailie H2. 161-162 þat shal be purposid]
is Rb. 162-163 a prelat . . . soulis] to prestes as prelatys pryncypally and
curates and oþur preistes þat Rb. 163 Frend] *om.* T, Hr, P. 164 how
entredist þou] *om.* Ht, P, T, Hr. 165 God . . . monye] *om.* U. 166 spirit]
gost T, Hr, P.—þou] *om.* A, H2; now Ht. 168 *add mg.* Noli negligere distere
T.—leerne] *add* for it is writen Noli negligere discere P.—clepid] called Rb.
169 ellis] *om.* Rb.
     Matthaeum 22] *om.* Ht, Ra, T, H9, U, Hu, P.

þat anoon folwiþ: "Byndiþ his hondis *and* his feet, *and*

(Matthaeum
22. 13)
þroweþ hy*m* i*n*to vttrewarde of derkenesses; þere shal be
wepyng *and* grynty*n*g of teþ." Þerfore y conseyle þe þat
þou avise þe how þou wilt answer*e* to þis questiou*n*: How
hast þou entrid? Wheþ*er* by clepi*n*g or by þyn owe*n* p*ro*-   175
curi*n*ge? For þou woldist t*r*auayle on Goddis gospell
oþer for þou woldest ben richelich arayed? Answer*e* to
þyn owe*n* co*n*science now as þou shalt or longe au*n*swer*e*
to God, þou þat hast take þe ordr*e* of p*r*est, wheþ*er*
þou be curat or no. Who stirid þe to take vpon þe so   180
hiȝe astaate? Wheþ*er* for þou woldest lyue on Goddis
co*n*templaci*o*n, oþer for to lyue a delic*i*ous lif vpon
oþer me*n*nis t*r*auayle *and* þyself t*r*auayle nouȝt?

   Why also sette*n* me*n* her*e* sones oþer her*e* cosynus   185
to scole? Wheþ*er* for to gete he*m* grete aua*u*nceme*n*t*is*
fol. 3ᵃ oþer to / make he*m* þe beter*e* to knowe*n* how þey shulde*n*

C
174 þou] *mg.* 175 or by] *of.* 181 for] *om.* 185 for] *om.*
Var
out 183-186 self . . . shulde*n* T.
171 folwiþ] suiþ Ht; *add* by þe gospell Rb, H9. 172 vttrewarde] vtter A;
vttere S; vtterest Rb, Ht, P; *add* plase Rb. 173 grynty*n*g] gnaistynge Rb, A,
H2. 175 þyn owe*n*] *om.* Rb. 176 Goddis] Cristes U. 177 ben] *add* wel and
P.—richelich arayed] ryched and worshipped here vppon vrthe Rb; *add* vpon
erþe H9. 178 owe*n* co*n*science] *om.* T, H9, Hr, P.—or longe] *om.* T, H9, Hr,
P. 179 p*r*est] prestehode Rb. 181-182 on Goddis co*n*templacion] *om.* T,
H9, Hr; *expunged* S. 181 lyue] *add* as a prest owiþ to doon in studie of
Goddis lawe to preche and teche and most hertili preie for þe puple H9, Hr,
mg. lh. S; as a prest ouȝt to in stondynge of Goddis lawes and to preche and
teche most hertilich pray for þe peple T, P. 184 oþer her*e* cosynus] *om.* Rb,
Ht; and here kyn U. 186 to make . . . shulde*n*] þat þei shuld knowe þe better
to Rb.—shulde*n*] *om.* A; *add* þe betere H9.

serue God? þis men may see openly by þe science þat þey
setten hem to. Why y praye ȝow putteþ men here sones
raþere to lawe syuyle *and* to þe kyngis court to writen
lettres or writis þan to philosophie oþer deuinite but   190
for þey hopen þat þyse ocupacions shul be euere menis to
make hem grete in þe world. I hope þat þer wole no man
seie þat þey ne shulde betere lerne reule of good lyuyng
in þe book of Goddis lawe þan in eny bokes of mennys
worldly wysdom. But certis now it is soþ þat Seynt Jon   195
Crisostome seiþ: Moderis beþ lowynge þe bodies of here
children, but þe soule þey dispiseþ. þey desireþ hem to
wel fare in þis world, *and* þey takeþ noon hede what þey
shul suffre on þat oþer. Summe ordeynen fees for here
childeren, but noon ordeynen hem to Godwar. þe lost of   200
þer bodies þey wolleþ dere bygge, but þe helþe of here
soule þe reccheþ nouȝt to take of ȝifte. Ȝif þey see
hem poore, þey sorweþ *and* sykeþ; but þouȝ þey see hem

*Omilia 27ª
operis
imperfectis*

C
202 see] *mg.*
Var
out T.
188 putteþ] sett Rb.—sones] kyn and here freendes U. 189 raþere] more Rb.
—syuyle] pleydable Rb.—court] bench Hr, H9, P; *add* to leerne U. 191 þyse]
swiche U.—euere] *om.* Ht, Hr, U; þe nexte Rb.—menis] *om.* A. 192-193 I
hope . . . þat] *om.* Rb. 193 ne shulde] where Rb.—good] Cristes Rb.—
lyuyng] *om.* H9. 195 certis] þerfore Rb.—soþ] ful soþ U. 196 Crisostome]
om. H9.—Moderis] lordis Ht; *add mg.* fadris Hu. 197 hem] *om.* H2.
199 oþer] *add* syde Hu.—Summe] *add* men U. 200 childeren] sonys Ht.—
lost] ese P. 202 reccheþ] ȝeue Rb.—to take of ȝifte] of Ht, Rb, Hr, P, U; to
take of heede A, Hu, H2. 203 hem poore . . . see] *om.* Hu.—and] *add* þei
H2, A.
    *Omilia . . . imperfectis] *om.* C, Ht, Ra, A, U, Hu, H2; omilia 28a H9;
omilia 28, operis imperfectis Rb; *mg. lh.* jon Crisomtom Ht, U.

synnen, þey sorwen nouȝt. *And* in þis þey sheweþ þat þey
brouȝten forþ þe / bodies but nouȝt þe soules.   205

And ȝif we taken hede trewly what abhominacions
ben scaterrid in þe chirche nowadayes among prestis, we
shulde wel wite þat þey alle comeþ nouȝt into þe folde of
Crist by Cristis clepynge for to profite but by oþer
weyes to gete hym worldly welþe; *and* þys is cause of   210
many errouris among þe puple. *And* herfore it is writen
in þe Book of Mornynge, where þe prophete spekeþ þus to
God: "þe enemye haþ put his hond to alle þyngis desirable
to hym, for he haþ seyn folk laweles entrid into þe
seyntewarie of þe wiche þou haddist coumaundid þat þey   215
shulde not entre into þy chirche." Þis enemye is Satanas,
as is name sowneþ, þat haþ put his hond to al þat hym
likeþ. What synne y praie ȝow wolde þe fend haue sowe
on men þat it nis now vsid? In what plente is pride,

fol. 3ʳᵇ (marginal, beside line 205)

*Threni 1º. (10) (marginal, beside line 210)

C
207 ben] *om.* 218 ȝow] *om.*
Var
out T. 206-219 Rb.
204 sorwen] make no sorowe Rb.—nouȝt] no þing Ht. 205 brouȝten forþ]
be parentes of Rb. 207 *add mg. lh.* priests reproved Ra.—ben] *om.* Hu; *lh.* S.
—nowadayes] þese dayes P. 208 folde] helpe P. 209 Crist] *mg.* Hu. 210
welþe] goedes Hr.—cause] *add* lesynge of soulis þat Crist bouȝte so dere and
H9; lesyng of soules þat God bouȝte from þe deþe and Hr, P. 211 many] *add*
grete Hu. 217 sowneþ] schewed Hr.—al] *add mg. lh.* þinges desirable to hym
þat is to alle Hu. 218 ȝow] *om.* S.—sowe] *om.* P. 219 what plente] prelacy
P, Hr.
    *Treni 1º] *om.* Ht, Hu; *add* Jeremie U.

enuye, wraþe, *and* coueytise! Whanne were þey so grete 220
as þey beþ now, *and* so of alle oþer synnes! *And* why
trowest þou but for þer beþ lawles peple entrid *into* þe
temple þat neyþer kepeþ *in* hemself þe lawe of God ne
kunne teche oþere. *And* to euerych suche seyþ God by þe
*Osee 4°. prophete Osee: "For þat þou hast put awey kunnynge, y 225
(6) shal putte þe awey þat þou shalt / vsen no presthod to
fol. 3ᵛᵃ me." Lo, þat God expressely here on holy writ forbediþ
men to take þe stat of presthod on hem but þey haue
kunnyng þat nedeþ hem. þou þan þat canst neyþer reule
þyself ne oþer aftir þe lawe of God, bewar how þou wolt 230
answere to God at his dredeful dom, whan he shal seye to
þe þat y tok to my teme: ȝelde rekenyng of þy balie how
þou hast entrid.

þe secunde questioun þat euery curat *and* prelat of
holy chirche shal answere to is þis: How hast þou reulid, 235

C
221 of] *om.* 229 þan] *om.*
Var
out Rb. 220-235 enuye . . . shal T.
223 temple] seyntuarie H9, Hr; *mg. lh.* S. 224 kunne] *add* not H2.—God by]
om. Ht. 225 Osee] *om.* H9.—y] *om.* A. 226 awey] *om.* Hr. 227 here . . .
writ] *om.* P. 229 þan] *om.* Hr, A, H2. 232 þat y tok to my teme] *om.* Hr, P.
232-233 how þou hast entrid] *om.* Ht, A, H2. 234-235 of holy chirche] *om.*
Hr, P.
　*Osee 4°] *in text* P.

þat is to seye þe soulis of þi suget*is and* þe goodis of
pore me*n*. ȝeue now þyn acou*n*te. First, how þou hast
gou*er*ned Goddis folk þat was take*n* þe to kepe? As an
herde ouþ*er* as an hyred ma*n* þat doþ al for þe loue of
his bodily hir*e*? As a fadir ouþ*er* as a wolf þat etiþ þe   240
shep *and* kepet he*m* nouȝt? Seye who*m* þou haast tu*r*ned fro
her*e* cu*r*sid lyuy*n*ge by þy deuout p*r*eching. Whom hast þou
tawth þe lawe of God þat was arst vnku*n*ny*n*ge? Þer shal
be*n* herd a greu*i*ous acusy*n*ge of fadirles childre*n and* an
hard alleggy*n*ge þat þey haue lyued by her*e* wa / ges *and*   245
not don awey her*e* syn*n*es. ȝelde also þe reke*n*y*n*ge how
þou hast reulid *and* spe*n*did þe goodis of por*e* me*n*.

Here what seiþ Seyn Bernard: "Dredeþ clerkis, dre*d*iþ
myn*is*tris of þe chirche þe whiche, *in* þe place of seynt*is*,
þat þey doþ so wickidly þat þey, noȝt holdy*n*ge he*m* apaied   250
wiþ swyche wagis þat wer*e* sufficiau*n*t to he*m*, þat ou*er*-
plus þat nedy me*n* sholde be susteyned by þey beþ not shamed

fol. 3ᵛᵇ (margin, line 245)

Bernardus super cantica sermone 23° (margin, line 248)

C
240 as a wolf] *om.* as.   246 þe] *ins. above.*
Var
out 236-237 þat is . . . acou*n*te Rb.   246-252 ȝelde . . . shamed Rb.
237 acou*n*te auctorite U, Hu.   238 As wheþer were þou T, Hr, P; wheþer
as H9.   239 ouþer as an hyred *om.* Ht.—þe loue of *om.* Rb, T, Hr, P, H2.
240 hire] *add* and sustynaunce P.—As] wheþir as Rb, H9, P; oþer as Hr.
241 whom] whanne S; *mg. lh.* whome S.   243 arst] before Rb, A, H2.
244 herd] *add* a grett noyss and Rb.   245 alleggynge] *add* aȝeyns þis curates
Rb; agens þese prestis H9.—þey] þe prestes T, Hr, P.—here] þise pore mens
Rb.   249 whiche] *add* byn Ht, S, H9; sitteþ A, H2.—seyntis] *add* beþ ȝe se T,
Hr, P.   250 þat þey doþ so wickidly] *om.* T, Hr, P.   251-252 ouerplus]
ouerpressech pore and Hr; ouere perise þe T; oppresseþ P.   252 men] *add*
and take awey her goodis þat þey T, Hr, P.—be susteyned by] han Ht.
   Bernadus . . . 23°] om. Hu, P; Bernardus Ht, T, U.

to waste in þe houses of here pride *and* here lecherie, *and*
wiþholdiþ to hemselue wickidly *and* cursidly þe liflode of
pore men. Wiþ dowble wickidnesse trewly þey synneþ;   255
first for þey reueþ oþer mennes goodes, *and* siþþe for þey
mysuse holy þyngis in here vanites *and* in here filþhedis."
Euerych such bailie þerfore bewar, for anoon to þe laste
ferþyng he shal rekene. Trowist þou not þanne þat þou ne
shalt be disalowid of God of þat þou hast dispendid in   260
fedynge of fatte palfreies, of hondes, of hawkes, *and*,
ȝif it so be þat is worst of alle, on lecherous wommen.

Job xxᵒ. (xxi. 13) Here what is seid of suche? "Þey haue lad here dayes in
welþe *and* in a poynt þey beþ go doun into helle." Þenk

fol. 4ʳᵃ þerfore, I rede, þat þou shalt ȝilde rekenynge / of þy   265
baylie.

Þe þridde questioun þat þis first baylife shal
answere to is þis: how hast þou lyued? What liȝt of holynesse hast þou shewid in þy lyuynge to þe puple, or what

C
260 of þat] *om.* of.
Var
out Rb.
253 houses] usis H9, A, H2. 255 synneþ] seyn Ht. 256 reueþ] reuen S; *mg.*
lh. rauind S; takeþ and bireueþ P. 257 *and in* here filþhedis] *om.* Ht. 258 þer-
fore] *om.* Ht.—anoon] *om.* U, A, H2. 259 rekene] *add mg. lh.* with Christ S.
—þanne] *om.* A, H2. 261 fatte palfreies] *om.* U. 263 lad] *add* alle A, H2.—
here] *add* lif in her T, Hr, P.—*in*] *add* lust and in Hr, P. 265 I rede] *om.* Hr.
      *Job xxᵒ] *om.* Ht, U, Hu; Job xxi Ra, S, T, H9, A, Hr, H2, *in text* P.

meroure hast þou be of holynesse to hem? ȝeue now þy reke-   270
nynge how þou hast lyued. As a prest oþer as a lewid man?
As a man or as a best? It is to wondry trewly how þe lif
of prestis is chaunged. þey beþ cloþed as knyȝtes; þey
speken as vnhonestly as cherlis, oþer of wynnynge as marchaundis; þey riden as princes; *and* al þis þat is þus spent   275
is of þe goodis of pore men *and* of Cristis heritages.

Hugo de Sancto Victore   Herfore seiþ an holy doctour: þe clay of Egipte was
touȝ, stynkynge, *and* medlid wiþ blood; þe sclattes weren
harde to be vndo, for þey were bake wiþ þe fier of coueytise *and* wiþ þe liȝe of lustis. In þise trauayleþ riche   280
men; in þise þey wakeþ awaytynge pore men; in þis trauayleþ prelatis þat beþ blente wiþ to myche schynynge of
richesses, þat makeþ hem housis lich chirches in gretnesse,
þat wiþ diuerse peyntoures colouren her chaumbres, þat wiþ
diuerse cloþynge of coloures makeþ ymagis gaye. But þe   285

C
271 oþer as a] *om.* as.   276   þe]*om.*
Var
out Rb.
270 hem] *add* þat ben as vnder þi cure ȝeue A, H2.   272 wondry] *add* vpon A,
H2.   273 prestis] presthod A, H2.   274 cherlis] seculeres *canceled* Hr;
rybaudys or cheerlys *mg.* Hr; clerkis T, P.   277 seiþ] *add* a grete clerk T, Hr,
P.   278 touȝ] þoruȝ T; þurgh Hr.   279 fier] cley A, H2.   284-285 chaumbres
. . . coloures] *om.* T, H9, P; *mg.* Hr.
    *Hugo . . . Victore] *om.* Ht, Hu; *in text* P; Augustinus U.

fol. 4ʳᵇ   pore man for defaute of cloþes beggeþ, *and* wiþ an emp / ti
wombe crieþ at þe dore. *And* ȝif y shal soþ seye, seiþ
þis doctour, ofte tymes pore me*n* be*n* robbed for to cloþen
wiþ trees *and* stones.

*Isaye xjᵒ.   To swiche spekeþ þe p*r*ophete Ysaye: "Hoo art þou here,   290
(xxii. 16)   or as who art þou her*e*?" Here þou art ocupienge þe place
of Petir, oþ*er* of Poul, oþ*er* of Thom*as*, oþ*er* of Martyn.
But how? As Judas was among þe apostelis, as Symound
Magus was amonge disciplis, as a candel newe queynt þat
stynkeþ al þe hous in stede of a lyȝt lanterne, and as a   295
smoke þat blendeþ mennys eiȝen *in* place of clier fier,
ȝif þou co*n*trarie þus þe forme of lyuynge þat Crist and
his apostelis lefte*n* to prestis. Þerfore seiþ þe prophete
*Jeremias   Jeremye: "Þey haueþ entrid, *and* þey haueþ had *and* not ben
xxxijᵒ.   obedient." Þey haueþ wiþ fals tytle oþer fals and corupt   300
(23)

Var
out Rb.
287 dore] gate H2.   291 or as who art þou here] *om.* Ht.   292 oþer of
Thom*as*, oþer of Martyn] et cetera Ht.   295 lyȝt] bryt Ht; cleer P.   296 place]
stede Ht, A, H2.—clier] cleene T, Hr.   297 of] *add* clene Ra.   298 apostelis]
disciplis T, Hr, P.—þerfore] lo what T, Hr, H9, P.   299 Jeremye] *om.* T, Hr;
Isaye P.   299-300 *and* þey . . . obedient] *om.* U.   300 haueþ] *add ins. above lh.*
enteryd H9; *add* had U, P; *add lh. ins. above* had Hu.
    *Isaye xjᵒ] *om.* Hu, H2; Isai Ht; Ysay 10ᵒ T, Hr, H9, *in text* P; Ysaie xxii
A, U.
    *Jeremias xxxijᵒ] *om.* Hu, P; Jeremi Ht, U; Isaias xxx T, Hr.

intencion, and þey haueþ had þore mennes goodis to here
mysvsyng, and þey haueþ not ben obedient to þe lawe of
God in here owne lyuynge. Þerfore it is writen þat "þe
hardeste dom shal fallen vpon suche;" an hard dom / for
þey haueþ mysentrid, an hardere dom for þey haueþ mysreulid   305
and þe hardeste dom for þey haueþ so cursidly lyued. Þenk
þerfore, y rede, how þou wolt ȝelde rekenynge of þy baylye.

Þe secunde baylif þat acounteþ at þis dom for hymself
and also for oþere is he þat kepynge haþ of eny comunyte,
as kynges, princys, maires, and schyreuys, and justices.   310
And þise schullen also answere to þe same þre questiouns.

Þe firste question: how hast þou entrid, þat is to
seye into þyn offis? Oþer for helpe of þe peple to des-
troie falshed and forþeren trewþe, oþer for desir of wyn-

Sapientia vjo. (6) fol. 4va (marginal note beside lines 3–4)

C
314 falshed] falsed.
Var
out 301-307 Rb. 302-314 haueþ . . . wyn-Hu.
301 intencion] *add* entred Hr, P.—and þey haueþ had] *om.* U; *add ins. above*
lh. and nouȝt ritfully Hr. 303 owne] lawe þe T; lawe þe *canceled* A; luþer P.
—lyuynge] lying Ht. 304 *add mg.* iudicium durissimum in hiis qui praesunt
T. 305 dom] *om.* Ht, A, H2. 306 so] *om.* Ht. 307 rede] *add* þee U.—ȝelde]
ȝeue S, A, H2. 308 *add mg. lh.* the second bailie H2.—acounteþ] acountes
shal ȝyue T, P, H2. 309 comunyte] covent P, T. 310 kynges] knyȝtes Rb,
U.—princys] *add* knyȝtis T, Hr, H9; *add* dukes, erles, barones, lords, knyȝtes
P.—schyreuys] squyes T. P, Hr.—justices] *add* and oþire souereynes of puplis
H9, Rb; *add* baillifs and oþer suche P. 311 þre] *add* same P. 312 question]
om. T, H9, Hr, P. 312-313 þat is to seye] *om.* Ht, Rb, H9, Hr, P, T.
313 offis] *add* oþur in astate Rb.—helpe] profyt Ht. 314 forþeren] support
Rb.—of wyn] *om.* Rb.
Sapientia vjo] om. U, P; Sapientia vijo Ra.

nyng oþer werldly worschip? "ȝif þat þou take such an offys

8° Ethi-
corum the-
marum 915ᵃ
fol. 4ᵛᵇ

more for þyn owne worldly profyt þan for helpe of þe comunyte, þou art a tirau*n*t," as þe phylosophre seyþ. For
it is to drede last þer ben manye þat desiren / suche
states þat þey may þe rapere oppresse þilke þat þey hateþ
and take ȝiftes to spare to punysche þilke þat haued
trespaced and so makeþ hem partineres of here sy*n*nes.
And many suche, whan þey beþ so heye, þey þenkeþ not þat
þey beþ pore me*n*nys breþreryn, but þey weneþ to passe hem
in kynde as þey passeþ *in* worldly worschipe, þat is but

Osee 8.
(4)

wynde. Of wheche God seiþ by þe prophete: "Þey haueþ
regned, but not of me; þey haueþ be princes, but I knowe
hem nouȝt."

II Para-
lipomenon
X. (1-19)

So we redeþ of Roboam þat was þe sone of Kyng Salamon. "What tyme he was first kyng þe puple of Israel comen

315

320

325

C
327 hem] *om.*
Var
out Hu
315 nyng] *om.* Rb; *add* or catel H9; *add* of catele Hr, P, T, (*part in margin*).—
an] *add* worldeli Ra.   316 worldly] *om.* A, H2.—profyt] *add* and wurchippe
Rb.—helpe] helþe Ht.   316-317 comunyte] covent T, P.   318 drede] *add* he
seiþ þat P; *mg. lh.* fear S.—last] *om.* T, Hr, P, H2; þat Ra, A.   319 states] *add*
hyȝ Rb.   319-320 þey hateþ . . . þilke] *om.* H9.   320 take] *om.* Rb.—to
punysche þilke þat haued] *om.* Rb.   321 so] *add* no doute of þei Rb; *add* no
doute he H9; þus þei T, Hr, P.—synnes] *add* and so shall be perceyners of
peynes Rb.   324 in kynde as þey passeþ] *om.* Ht.—worldly] vayn Rb.   325
wheche] such Rb, A, H2.   329 What tyme he was first kyng] *om.* H9.—he
was first kyng] he shuld regne Rb.
    8° Ethicorum . . .] om. Ht, Ra, U; *in text* P.
    Osee 8] om. Ht, Ra, H2; *in text* P.
    II Paralipomenon x] om. Ht, T, P; *lh.* II Paralipomenon xx S; 2 Parali-
pomenon 8 Rb; Roboas tertia Regum xij° capiter U.

to hym and seyden: þy fadre in his laste dayes putte vpon   330
vs a gret charge. We prayeþ þat þou wole sumwhat make
it lyȝttere, and we wole serue þe. And þe / kyng tok
consel of þe olde wise men, *and* þey conseileden hym to
answere hem fayre, *and* þat shulde be for þe beste. But
he lefte þis olde wise me*nnis* conseyl, *and* dide aft*ir* þe   335
conseyl of children þat weren his pleiferen, *and* seyde
to þe peple wha*n* þey come*n* aȝe*n*: My lest fyngere is
grettere þa*n* my fadres rygge; my fadir greued ȝow su*m*-
what, but y wole eken more. *And* þe peple herden þis, *and*
rebelledyn to hy*m*, *and* toke he*m* anoþer kyng. *And* siþe   340
come neuere þe kyngdom aȝeen hool."

And þerfore it is good þat euery lowere of comunytes
þat þey be not lad be foolis ne be none ere rowneres
þat he ne haue an eyȝe of loue to þe comynite þat he haþ

C
330 and seyden] *add* to hym.   333 hym] *om.*   335 wise] *om.*
Var
out   330-339 to hym . . . peple Hu.
330 seyden] *add* to hym Ra, T, Hr, H9; *add* sir Rb; *add* þus A, H2.   331 sum-
what] *om.* Ht; some dele S.   332 wole] *add* gladly Rb.—tok] lyuynge þe Rb.
333 *and* þey] þat Rb.   334 hem] þe pepull Rb; *om.* Hr, P.—fayre] *add* and
plesauntly Rb.   334-335 *and* þat shulde . . . conseyl] *om.* Rb.—dide aftir]
toke Rb.   336 children] ȝonge men Rb.   336-337 *and* seyde . . . aȝen] to
ȝyff þis answere þat was þis Rb.   338 rygge] *om.* T, P; *add* bon H9; *add* thy P.
339 but y wole eken more] and ȝit wolle I greue ȝow and eken hit more T, Hr,
P.—more] *add* þer to S, A, H2; *add* þan whan Rb.   339-340 *and* rebelledyn to
hym] þe putt hym downe Rb.   340 to] aȝens Ht.—siþe] *om.* Rb.   341 hool]
add togydere Ht.   342 euery] *om.* Rb.—lowere] leders Rb, A, U, H2; lorde
Ht; reuler T, Hr, H9, P; lawere or ruler Hu.—comunytes] coventys T, P; *add*
be wys and P; *add mg.* be he lord or kyng Hr.   343 none] *om.* Ra, Rb; *add*
oþer Ht, S, Hr, U, Hu.—ere] hyer T; hye P.—rowneres] willes P.   344 haue]
add alwey P.—of loue] *om.* A, H2.—loue] donward P; *add* doune T, Hr.

to reule. For wyte he wel, be he neuere so hiȝ, þat he   345
shal come byfore his heiȝere to ȝelde þe rekenyng of his
bayle.

þe secunde questioun: how hast þou rewlid,
þat is to seye þe peple *and* þe office þat þou haddist
to gouerne? þou þat hast ben a juge in causis of pore   350
men, how hast þou keped þis hest of God? "þou schalt not

Leviticus   take hede of þe persone of a pore man to be to hym þe
xix. (15)   hardere for his pouert"; ne þou schalt not beholde a
riche mannis semblaunt to spare oþer to fauoure hym in
wrong for his richesse.   355

fol. 5ʳᵇ   O Lord God, what abusioun is þer among officeres /
of here boþe lawes nowadayes. ȝif a gret man plete wiþ
a pore to haue owt þat he holdeþ, euerich officer schal
be redy, al þat he may, *and* hiȝe þat þe riche man myȝt
haue suche an ende as he desireþ. But ȝif a pore man   360
plede wiþ a riche man, þan þer schal be so many delayes

C
350 þou þat] þat þou.   361 þer] þat oþer.
Var
346 heiȝere] gretter T, Hr, P.   347 bayle] baylyeshippe Rb.   349 þat is to
seye] *om.* Ht, T, Hr, H9, P.   351 how] *om.* A, H2.   352 hede] *mg.* Hr.—be to
hym] *lh. ins. above* Hu.   354 to spare oþer] *om.* Rb.   356 God] *om.* S, U.
358 pore] *add* man Rb, S, A, Hu, H2.—euerich] *om.* Rb; *add* man Hu.
359 *and* hiȝe] to fulfill Rb.   359-360 myȝt . . . desireþ] desyre Rb.   360 an
ende] sped P.   361 þer] þat oþer Ra, A, S.
   Leviticus xix] *om.* U, Hu; Deuteronomium S, T, *lh.* Ht.

þat, þou3 þe pore mannes ri3t be open to al þe comite,
for pure faute of spendyng he shal be glad to cese.
Schirreues *and* ballies wolleþ retorne pore mennes writ*is*
wiþ *tarde venit* but þey felen mede i*n* her handes. *And*   365
3it y here men seye, þat han asayed boþe lawes, þat
þilke court þat is clepud *Cristen* court is moche more
Proverbia cursed. þerfore it is write: "3iftes þey take owt of
xvij. (23)   mennes bosomes to ouerturne þe weyes of ri3t dom." But
Matthaeum it is to drede þe word of Crist: "I*n* what dom 3e demeþ   370
vij. (2)   3e schulleþ be demed" whan 3e come*n* to 3elde rekenyng of
3our*e* baylie.

    þe þrid q*u*estiou*n* is: How hast þou liued, þou þat
demest *and* punysschist oþer men for her t*r*espas? A
Rabanus grete doctou*r* seiþ: þe behoueþ to flee þe wikkednesse   375
of oþer men þat þou chastisest for her*e* trespacis. For

C
371 3elde] *om.*
Var
362 be ope*n* to al] neuer so openly knowen in Rb.—to al þe comite] knowyn
P.—comite] cuntre Ht, Ra, Rb, U, Hu, H2; comente T, Hr, H9, A. 363 shal]
mg. Hr; is T, P.—glad] fayn Rb.—cese] fall from is owne ry3th for Rb; *add*
and so leseþ his ry3t for P. 365 þey felen] þer fall Rb; þey wul P.—mede i*n*
her handes] in her fyngers som maner of mede Rb; meden hem P. 366 3it]
om. A, H2.—asayed] seen Ht; sel3en S. 367 *Cristen* court] *om.* court Ht, S.
—moche] *om.* Ht, Hu. 368 cursed] *add* what for sounynge and sensures of
symonbys children all þe sothe may not be said þat man seyþ at eie Rb.—
3iftes] *lh. ins. above* Hr. 370 *Crist*] *add* þat seith U; *add* seiþ P. 370-
371 demeþ 3e] deed men U. 371 3elde] *om.* Ra; 3yue P. 374 demest *and*]
om. U, Hu.—her] *add* lyuynge and Rb.
    Proverbia xvij] *om.* U, Hu; Pro. 13 *lh.* Ht; Pro. xv T; *in text* P.
    Matthaeum vij] *om.* C, Ra, Rb, T, Hr, A, U, Hu, P; *lh.* Ht; Math *lh.* S.
    Rabanus] *om.* C, Ht, Ra, T, H9, U, Hu, P.

ʒif þyself do vnlawfulliche in demynge oþer men, þou dampnest þyself siþ þou dost þat þou dampnest. *And* Poul seiþ:
"Whi techist þou not þyself þat techist oþere; why stelist
þou þat techist not oþer men to stele?" Seynt Gregory   380
seiþ: "He schal not take gouernayl of oþere þat can-
/ not go byfore hem in good lyuynge." *And* whan any man
stant byfore hym in dom, he most take hede tofore what
Juge he shal stonde hymself to take his dom aftir his
dedis.   385

But it is to drede þat many fareþ as þe tweye false
prestis þat wolde haue dampned to deþ holy Susanne, for
sche nolde nouʒt assente to here lecherie. Of whiche it
is writen: "þey turneden awey here eiʒen, for þey wolde
not se heuene ne haue mynde of ryʒtful dom."   390
So it happiþ ofte þey þat were more worþy to be honged
dampneþ hem þat beþ lasse worþy. As a clerk telleþ of
Socrates þe philosofre: Vpon a day a man axkid of hym
why he leyʒede; *and* he seyde, for y see grete þeues lede
a litil þef to hongynge. Y preie ʒe, wheþer is he þe   395

Marginal notes (left column):
*Romanos ij. (21)
*25 moralium in fine
fol. 5ᵛᵃ
*Daniel xiij. (9)
*Valerius Maximus libro vijᵒ

C
381 not] *om.* 395 ʒe] *om.—*he] *om.*
Var
378 siþ þou dost þat þou dampnest] *om.* A, H2.—*And*] *add* Seynt P, A, H2.
380 men] *add* þat þei shuld Rb. 380-385 Seynt . . . dedis] *om.* Rb. 381 not]
om. Ra, S, U, Hu.—He schal not] how schal he Ht. 382 go byfore] gouerne
T, Hr, P. 386 is] *mg. lh.* S.—þat] lest T, H9, Hr, P. 387 holy] *add* whomman
Ht. 388 lecherie] lecherous desyr Hr, P. 393 philosofre] *add* saiþ S.
395 ʒe] *om.* H9, A, H2.
*Romanos ij] *om.* C, Ra, H9, A, Hu, P; *lh.* Rom. Ht; Paulus Rb, U; tu qui
alios doces te ipsum non doces T, Hr.
*25 moralium in fine] *om.* Rb, Hu; Gregorius Ht, U, *in text* P.
*Daniel xiij] *om.* Ht, A, Hr, U, Hu; Daniel C; avertunt oculos T.
*Valerius Maximus libro vijᵒ] *om.* U, Hu, *in text* P; Socrates Rb, *lh.* Ht.

grettere þef þat bynemeþ a man his hous *and* his lond fro
hym *and* from his eyres for euermore oþer he þat for makynge
of a gret nede steleþ a schep oþer a calf? Wheþer trowe
ȝe now þat it happe suche extorcioneris to be oþer-wile
juges *and* deme men þus to deþ. But y rede þe þat þus   400
demest oþer þynke on þat dom þat þou shalt come to ȝelde
rekenyng of þy balie.

    þe þridde bailif þat schal be cleped to þis dredful
acounte schal be euery Cristene man þat schal rekene to
his Lord God for þe goodis þat he haþ had of hys. / *And*   405
here y wole speke but of þe firste questioun, þat is þis:
How entredist þou? *And* here bewar, ȝee þat haueþ geten
any worldly good, oþer take by extorciones, by raueyne,
by vsure, oþer by disceit. Woo shal be to þe at þis dred-

fol. 5ᵛᵇ

C
401 to ȝelde] to to ȝelde þe.
Var
396 bynemeþ] takis awey Rb; revyþ A, H2.   397-398 makynge of a] *om.* Ht,
Rb, T, Hr, P.   398 gret] *om.* Rb.—calf] dowe Rb.—Wheþer] *om.* Rb.   399
ȝe] we S, U, Hu, A, H2.—now] not Ht, Rb, S, H9, U, Hu, A, H2.—oþer-wile]
add among T; *add* among þe peple P.   399-400 to be oþer-wile juges *and*]
om. Rb.   400 men] þe lesse peuys Rb, H9.—to deþ] *om.* S; *add* ȝe certeyn I
trowe T, Hr, P.   400-401 But y . . . oþer] take hede man and Rb.   401 oþer]
þat þu A, H2.   402 balie] bayliffshipp Rb.   403 *add mg. lh.* the thrydd baile
H2.   404 acounte] reckenyng A, H2.—euery] *om.* A.—to] *add* fore T, Hr, P.
408 worldly good] good wrongfully Ht, A, H2.   409 vsure] *add* by fals
chafferynge Rb, H9.—by disceit] by any deceit Rb, H9.—þe] all suche Rb.

*Augustin-
us de ver-
bis domini.
capitulo
xx°*

ful day. As Seynt Austen seyþ: "ʒif he be cast into þe   410
fier þat haþ nouʒt ʒeuen of his owne good, where trowest
þou he schal be cast þat haþ reued oþer mennes from hem?
And ʒif he schal brenne wiþ þe fend þat haþ nouʒt cloþed
þe nakede, where trowest þou schalt he brenne þat haþ

*Gregorius
iij° Mora-
lium. capi-
tulo viij*

maad hym nakid þat was erst cloþed?" But as Seynt Gregory   415
seyþ: "To þyngis makeþ men to lyue þus by raueyne of þer
neiʒebores: þat beþ desir of hyeʒnesse, *and* drede of
pouerte."

And what vengeaunce falliþ of þis synne of coueytise

*Zacharias
vj°. (v.
5-11)*

y may se by figure in holy writ, "whan þe aungel seide to   420
þe prophete Zacarie: Rere vp þyn eiʒen *and* see what is þat
þat goþ owt. *And* þe prophete seyde: What is it? Þan
þe aungel seyde: Þis is þe pot goynge owt; þis is þe

C
414 he] *ins. above.*   421 þat] *om.*
Var
410 day] reknyng U.   411 good] *add* no þyng P.   412 reued] *add* oþur
begyles Rb.—mennes] *add* goodis Ht, Rb, T, A, Hr, U.   414 nakede] *add*
men A, H2.   415 erst] first A, H2.   417 þat] þe whiche A, H2.—þat beþ]
om. Rb.—desir of] *add* richis and T, Hr, P.—drede of] *add* worldes Rb.   419
falliþ] comeþ H9.   420 y] ʒee Ht.—se] shew Rb, T, Hr, P.—whan] wherer A,
H2.   421-422 is þat þat] *om.* T, H9, P; *mg.* Hr.
     *Augustinus . . .] *om.* Ht, U, Hu; *lh.* Ra; *in text* P.
     *Gregorius . . .] *om.* U, Hu; *lh.* Ra; Gregorius Ht; *in text* P; iij Moralium
capitulo viij H2.
     *Zacharias vj°] *om.* Hu; *in text* P; Zacharias v H9, A, U, H2.

eiȝe of hem on al þe erþe. *And* þere was a whiȝt of led
ybore, *and þer* was a wo*mm*an sitta*n*de i*n* þe myddel of þis   425
pot. *And* þe au*n*gel seyde: Þis is impiete. *And* he tok
her*e and* cast here i*n*to þe myddle of þe pot, *and* he tok
þe gobet of led *and* keste it i*n*to þe pottis mouþ. *And*
þe p*r*ophete lifte vp his eiȝe*n*, *and* he saye to wo*mm*en

fol. 6ʳᵃ   co / my*n*ge owt *and* spirit*is* in here wyng*is*. *And* þey hadde   430
wynges lik to kites oþer gledis. *And* þey rered vp þis pot
bytwyn heuene *and* erþe. *And* þa*n* þe p*r*ophete spak to þe
au*n*gel: Whider wole þese bere þis pot? *And* he seyde:
I*n*to þe lond of Sennar."

    Þis pot is coueytise. For ryȝt as a pot haþ a wid   435
ope*n* mouþ, so coueytise eu*er*emore gapiþ aft*ir* worldly
goodis. *And* ryȝt as þe licour in þe pot p*r*ofiteþ not to
þe pot but to me*n* þat drawe*n and* drynkeþ þerof, so worldly goodis ofte p*r*ofiteþ not to chynchis but to oþere þat

C
439 ofte] *om.*
Var
426 Þis is] þat she was Rb. 428 þe gobet] þis weyȝt P. 430-431 *And* þey
hadde wynges] *om.* S. 431 kites oþer] *om.* A, H2.—oþer gledis] *om.* Ht, P; to
puttokys Rb.—rered] lifte Rb. 432 heuene] hem Rb. 433 aungel] *add* and
asked hym Rb.—þese] *add* wommen A, H2.—he] þe aungel P. 434 Sennar]
mg. lh. S. 435 pot] *om.* U. 436 ope*n*] *om.* Ht, T, P; *ins. above* Hr.—euere-
more] *om.* S. 437 profiteþ] *add canceled* wordliche goodes Hr. 438 drawe*n*]
vsyn it T, Hr, H9, P; *om.* Rb.—*and* drynkeþ] *om.* Ht, T, Hr, H9, P.—so] *add
canceled* to oþer þat comeþ after Hr. 439 chynchis] negardes Rb; *add mg.
lh.* churles S.

Ecclesias-   comeþ aftir. As it is write: "He þat haþ moneye shal haue   440
tes sexto.
(v. 9)   no fruyt of hit." *And* þis coueytise is þe eize of coueytouse men. For þey beþ blynde to see how þey shulle go
to heuene, but to wynnyng of worldly þyng þey seeþ many
weies lik to owles *and* nytcrowes þat seen betre be ny3t
þan by day.   445

    Þe gobet of led is þe synne of obstinacion. Þe wom-
man sittynge in þe pot is vnpite, as þe aungel seyde,
þat folweþ auarice. For þurgh auarice a man leseþ þe pite
þat he schulde haue of þe myschef of his sowle siþ ofte
men lesiþ þe lif of here sowle by dedly synne þat þey   450
doiþ to haue wynninge. *And* also þey leseþ þe pite þat
þey schulde haue to here body, puttynge hemself to many
grete bodily trauayles *and* perilis, boþe of se *and* of
fol. 6rb   lond, *and* al makeþ coueytise. Þis pot / is stoppid wiþ
þe gobet of led whan vnpite is þus by synne of obstina-   455
cion closid in coueytise þat he may not go owt of þe

C
440 haþ] *om.* 443 seeþ] eþ *ins. above.* 449-450 siþ ofte . . . sowle] *lower mg.*
452 many] *add* to.
Var
440 haþ] *om.* Ra; kepiþ T, Hr, H9, P. 441 coueytise] *om.* Ht. 441-442 *And*
þis coueytise . . . men] *om.* P. 442 go] come Ht; se to goo S. 443 wynnyng]
þingis T.—þyng] goodes Rb; wynnyng T, þynynges Hr. 444 weies] þingis
H2. 448 auarice] *canceled, add* unri3twysnes S.—þurgh auarice] *om.* Rb.
449 ofte] *add* 3e seeþ P. 449-450 siþ ofte . . . sowle] *om.* Rb. 450 by]
þurwe P.—dedly] þis Rb.—synne] *om.* H2. 450-451 þat þey doiþ] *om.* P.—
þat þey . . . *And*] *om.* Rb. 451 haue] *add* worldlich T, Hr, H9, P; *mg. lh.* S.—
wynninge] *add* of þe world A, H2. 452 haue] *add* of þe myscheffe þat þei
shuld haue Rb. 453 grete] *om.* P.—*and* perilis] *om.* A, H2.—boþe] *mg.* Ra.
454 lond] *add* and also þei lese þe pite þat þei shuld haue of þe pore nedye þat
God haþ lymetyd þe boodes to Rb, H9.—coueytise] *add* and auarice Rb, H9.
455 gobet] *mg. lh.* S. 455-456 obstinacion] hardholdyng T, P; *mg.* Hr; *add*
oþer of hardholdyng Hr.
   Ecclesiastes sexto] *in text* P; *om.* U, Hu, H2; Ecclesiastes v T, *lh.* Ht.

*Job xx°
capitulo.
(22)
chynches hertes by penaunce. As Job seiþ: "Whan he is
fulfillid, he schal be stoppid."

Þe tweye wommen þat baren vp þis pot beþ pride *and*
*Proverbia
xxx. (15)
lust of flesch, þat beþ clepid in holy writ "þe tweye dowȝ-   460
tren of þe waterleche criyng: "Bryng, bryng." *And* þey
hadden wengis. Þe firste woman, þat is pride, haþ tweye
wengis. Þe firiste wenge is grace spiritual, as cunnynge,
wisdom, *and* conseyl, *and* many oþere, for whiche ȝiftes
ofte men wexiþ proude. Þe secunde wenge is bodily grace,   465
as strengþe, fayrhed, gentrie, *and* oþer suche, of whiche
men wexeþ proude ofte. Þe wengis of þe secunde womman,
þat is fleschly desir, beþ glotonye *and* slewþe. Of glotonye spekeþ Seynt Gregory: "Whan þe wombe is fulfillid,
þe prikkes of lecherie beþ meued." *And* of slewþe seiþ   470

C
462-463 þe firste woman þat is pride haþ tweye wengis] *om.*
Var
457 chynches] neggardes Rb.—penaunce] *add* of for þinkynge Hu.   459 þe
tweye] by twene þe S.—pride] couitise T, P, *written over an erasure* Hr.   460
clepid] cald Rb.   462-463 þe firste woman . . . wengis] *om.* Ht, Ra, Rb, A,
T, H9, H2; *mg. lh.* Hr.—woman is pride *canceled* S.   464-465 for whiche
. . . men] for which ȝyfte many other *mg. lh.* S.   465 ofte] *add* tyme T, Hr, P.
466 of whiche] where of *mg. lh.* S.   467 ofte] *om.* Rb; *add* tyme P.   468
desir] *add* is to sey Rb; þe whiche A, H2.
     *Job xx° capitulo] *om.* Hu; Job Ht, U, P; Job 22 Rb; Job 20 vel 22 H9.
     *Proverbia xxx] *om.* C, Ht, Ra, S, T, H9, A, U, Hu, P, H2.

*Augustinus
de conflic-
tu viciorum
et virtutum
Seynt Austen: "Loth, wil he in bysinesse dwellynge among
schrewes in Sodome, he was a good man; but whan he was
in þe hil slow for sikernesse, he in his dronkynschipe
lay by his doutren." *And* þese wommen hadden wengis lik to

*Bartholo-
meus liber
12, capitu-
lo 27
kitis, "þat wiþ a criynge vois sekeþ here mete," as Bartho-   475
lomeus seiþ.

And þus fareþ coueytise of men, witnessyng Seynt

*Augustinus
de verbis
domini
Austyn: "What is þe gredynesse of fleschly desir siþ
rauenes fisches haueþ sum mesure. Whan þey hungreþ, þey
rapeþ; but whan þey beþ fulle, þey spareþ. Only couey-   480

fol. 6ᵛᵃ
tise of men may not be fulfillid. Euere he takiþ / *and*
neuere haþ ynow. Neuere he dredeþ God ne schameþ men.
He ne spareþ fadir, ne knowiþ moder, ne acordeþ wiþ broþer,
ne kepeþ trowþe to his frend. He oppresseþ wydues *and*
harmeþ moderles children. Fre men he makeþ bonde, *and*   485

C
474 his] *mg.*
Var
471 *mg.* Genesis 19 H2, *lh.* A.   472 Sodome] *add* cite P.   473 sikernesse]
bisynesse Ra.—dronkynschipe] *add* made hym þat he A, H2.   474 his] *add*
two P.   475 kitis] gledes A, H2.—vois] *om.* H2; *add* went Rb.   478 Austyn]
add þat seiþ þus P; *add* and seys Rb.—gredynesse] gretenesse Ht, S, A, H2.
479 rauenes] ranknesse P; raven and A, H2.   479-480 Whan þey . . . þey
spareþ] *om.* H9.   480 Only] But Rb, T, P, Hr; But only A, H2, U.   481 not]
neuer Rb, H9.—he takiþ] þei couett Rb.   482 Neuere he] neiþir he Ht, T,
H9, Hr, U, Hu, A, H2; he Rb; he ne P.—ne] *add* þei be not Rb.—men] *om.*
Rb.   484 ne kepeþ . . . frend] *om.* Rb.
    *Augustinus . . . virtutum] *om.* H9, Hu, T, P; Augustinus Ht, U.
    *Bartholomeus . . . 27] *om.* Ra, T, Hu; *lh.* A; *in text* Rb; *in text* 2 libro
capitulo 12 P.
    *Augustinus . . . domini] *om.* Ht, Ra, Rb, S, T, H9, A, H2, Hr, U, Hu, P.

bryngeþ forþ fals wittenesse, *and* occupieþ dede me*n*nys
þy*n*gis, as þey shulde neu*er*e dye. What ma*n*hede is þis,"
seiþ þis docto*ur*, "þus to lese lyf of *grace and* gete deþ
of soule? Wy*n*ne gold, *and* lese heuene?" *And* herfor*e*

*Psalmo
liv. (11)*
seyþ þe p*r*ophete: "Trauayle i*n* þe middes þ*er*of *and* vnriȝtwisnesse."   490

*Innocen-
tius* de
vilitate
condicionis
hu*m*ane
Also I*n*nocent, speky*n*ge of þe harmes þat han come
of coueytise, seiþ þ*us:* "O how many me*n* haþ coueytise
disseyued *and* spilt. Of coueytise þat Balaha*m* wolde, for

*Numeri
xxii.
(15-25)*
ȝiftes þat þe kyng p*r*ofrede hym, haue ac*ur*sid Goddis   495
*Josue
vij°.
(21-25)*
peple; his oune asse r*e*prouede hym *and* hurt his foot to-
ȝenes þe walle. Achor was stoned, for coueytise made hy*m*
to stele gold *and* cloþes aȝen*is* þe comau*n*ment of God.

*4 Regum
5°. (20-27)*
Gyeȝy was smyte w*iþ* meselrye, for he solde a ma*n*nes helþe
þat cam of Goddis g*r*ace. Judas for coueytise solde C*r*ist   500

C
496 hym] *om.*
Var
487 þyngis] goodis Ht, Hu.   490 *and*] *add* vseþ T, P.   490-491 seyþ . . .
vnriȝtwisnesse] *om.* Rb.   494 wolde] hadde and T, Hr, P.   495 kyng] *add*
Balach Rb.—hym] *add* he wolde T, Hr, P.   497 walle] *add* as it is writen P.—
stoned] *add* to þe deþ Rb, T, H9, Hr, P, *mg. lh.* S.   498 comau*n*ment of God]
Goddes byddyng Rb.   499-500 he solde . . . *grace*] takynge ȝifte of Naaman
Rb.   499 a ma*n*nes] Naamannes A, H2.—helþe] heele A, H2.
    Psalmo liv] om. Ra, Rb, T, H9, Hr, U, Hu, P.
    *Innoce*n*tius . . . hu*m*ane] *om.* Ra, A, H2, Hu; Innocent Ht, U.
    Numeri xxii] om. C, Ht, U, Hu; *in text* P.
    Josue vij°] om. Ht, U, Hu; Iosue v T, Hr, *in text* P.
    4 Regum 5°] om. Ht, Ra, U, Hu; *in text* P.

(Mattaeum xxvii. 3-5). *Actus 5º. (1-11)

*Ecclesias- tici viijº

fol. 6ᵛᵇ

*3 Regum 21. (1-16)

and aftirward heng hymself. Ananye *and* Saphira his wyf
weren dede sodeynly, for þey forsoke to Petir her monye
þat þey hadden."

　　And coueytise makeþ also þat riche men etiþ þe pore,
as bestis don here leswes, holdynge hem lowe. Þis may　　505
we see in dede al day, I drede. / For ȝif a riche man
haue a feld *and* a pore man haue in þe myddis or in
þe syde þerof oon acre, or ȝif a riche man haue al a
strete saue oon hous þat sum pore broþer of hys oweþ,
he cesseþ neuere into þat he gete þat out of þe pore mannys　　510
hondis oiþer by prayere, oiþer by byggynge, oiþer by pursuynge.

　　Þus ferd it by Kyng Achab, þat þurw his fals quenes
engyn slow þe pore man Nabyoth, for he wolde nouȝt sille
hym his vyneȝerd þat was nyȝ to þe kyngis pales. Vpon　　515

C
508 þe] *om.*   513 by] *add* a.
Var
502   sodeynly] *mg.* Hu; *add* for coueitise Hu.   503 þat þey hadden] *om.* Rb.
504 pore] *add* as it is written P.   505 don] eetyn Ht, P; *om.* A, H2.   506 in
dede] *om.* T, Hr, H9, P.—I drede] *om.* Rb.   507 feld] *add* oþur a grett parte
of a towne Rb.—myddis] *add* þerof Ht.   507-509 in þe myddis . . . oweþ] an
acre of lond amonge is, oþur an hous, oþur a garden, anon hym þenkes þis
fell well for hym Rb.   509 strete] *add* holly P.—pore] *om.* Ht, S; *add* man a A,
H2.—oweþ] haþ Hr; *add* to haue Hu.   510 into þat] *add* tyme þat U; *mg.* Hr.
—þe pore mannys] is Rb.   511 oiþer by byggynge] *om.* S; *add mg. lh.* or by
buig S; *add* or chaunchyng Rb.   511-512 pursuynge] *add* oþur harmynge
hym with beestis or oþurwise Rb; *add* or chaffarynge or harmynge him wiþ
hise beestis or ony oþirwise H9; *add mg. lh.* of deceipt S.   513 ferd] *add*
somtymes P.—Kyng] *add* þat het T, Hr, P.—quenes] *mg.* Hr; *add* owne T;
add owne *canceled* Hr; *add* owne wyfes P.   513-515 þurw his . . . pales] þat
for coueitise þe pore mans vineȝerde Nabothe, for it was nyþ is paleys and for
he wold not sell it hym. Þerfore by þe fals quens counsell Jesabell he was
slayn, wherefore on hem bothe fell grett veniaunce Rb.   515 to þe kyngis] his
Ht.
　　*Actus 5º] *om.* Ht, U, Hu; Actus 8 T, Hr, *in text* P.
　　*Ecclesiastici viijº] *om.* Ht, Rb, T, Hr, Hu, P; Isaie v U.
　　*3 Regum 21] *om.* Ht, Rb, T, U, Hu, P.

*Ambrosius,
suo libello
de Nabioth
pauperis

whiches processe þus seiþ Seynt Ambrose: "How fer wole
ȝe riche men strecche ȝoure coueytise. Wole ȝe dwelle
alone vpon þe erþe *and* haue no pore man wiþ ȝow? Why
putte ȝe out ȝowre felawe in kynde *and* chalangeþ to
ȝoureself þe possessioun comune by kynde. In comune to   520
alle, riche *and* pore, þe erþe was maad. Why wole ȝee
riche men chalenge propre ryȝt herinne? Kynde knowiþ no
richessis, þat bryngeþ forþ alle men pore. For we beþ
nouȝt gete wiþ riche cloþis, neiþer bore wiþ gold ne wiþ
siluer. Ynakid he bryngeþ vs in to þe world, nedy of mete,   525
cloþynge *and* drynke. Nakid þe erþe takeþ vs as sche nakid
brouȝte vs hider. Sche cannouȝt close wiþ vs oure pos-
sessionis in þe sepulcre. Kynde makeþ no difference bytwyn pore *and* riche in comyng hidre, neiþer in goynge
hennes. Alle oon in a maner he bryngeþ forþ; alle oon   530

fol. 7ʳᵃ   in a manere he closeþ / in þe graue. Whoso makeþ dif-

Var
519-520 *and* chalangeþ . . . comune by kynde] *om.* Ht, T, P; *mg.* Hr.   521
alle] *om.* T, Hr, Hu, P; *add* men Ht, A, H2.—riche *and* pore] *om.* Hu.   522
herinne] here Rb, P; heere on eerthe U.   524 gete] born P.—bore] *om.* Ht,
P; brouȝt forþ S; *lh.* bore S.   525 he] kynde T, Hr, P.   528 sepulcre] graaue
U, Rb; *add* for T, P, H9, Hr.   529 pore] *add* men A, H2.   530 Alle oon . . .
forþ] *om.* Ht, Rb, A, H2, U; *mg.* Hr.   530-531 Alle oon . . . graue] *om.* Rb.
531 graue] *mg. lh.* Ht; *add* boþe riche and pore A, H2.—Whoso] þou þat A,
H2.
    *Ambrosius . . . pauperis] *om.* T, H9, Hu, P; Ambrosius U; Ambrose *lh.*
Ht.

ference of pore *and* riche abide al for to þey haue leye
a litel wile i*n* þe gr*a*ue, *and* þa*n*ne opene, *and* loke amo*n*g
dede bones who was riche *and* who was pore, but ȝif it be
wiþ þis: þ*at* moo cloþes roteþ wiþ þe riche þ*an* wiþ þe   535
pore. *And* þ*at* harmeþ to he*m* þ*at* beþ on lyue, *and* pro-
fiteþ not to þe dede." Þis seiþ þe docto*ur* of suche
extorcione*r*es. It is write*n:* "Oþ*er* me*n*nes feld þey repeþ,
and þe vyne of hym þ*at* þey haueþ oppressid þey plukkiþ
awey þe grapes. Þey leeueþ me*n* nakid, *and* takeþ awey   540
here cloþes, þ*at* haueþ not werwiþ to hile he*m* i*n* cold."
 " 'And þey lefte*n* vp þis pot bytwene heuene *and* erþe,'
for coueytouse me*n* neiþ*er* haue charite to he*re* breþ*er*e*n*
vpon erþe neiþ*er* to God in heuene. 'And þey bar þis pot
into þe lond of Sennar,' þ*at* is to seye i*n*to þe lond of   545
stench," þ*at* is helle. For "þ*er* schal be stench i*n* stede
of soote smellynge," as Ysaye seiþ. Be war, y rede, þat

(margin:) *Job xxiiij°. (6-7)*

(margin:) (Gregory)

(margin:) *Ysaye 3°. (23)*

C
539 haueþ] harmeþ.
Var
532 pore] *add* men A, H2.—abide] *add* a lytel while til A, H2; *add* til þe tyme
þat U; *add* tylle þey Hr.—haue] *add* both A, H2.   535 riche] *add* man T, Hr,
P, A, H2.   535-536 þan wiþ þe pore] *om.* Rb; *add* man T, Hr, P.   536 he*m*
þat beþ on lyue] þe lyffyng man Rb.   539 haueþ] harmeþ Ra, S, A, H2.—
plukkiþ] pulleþ T, Hr, P.   541 here . . . cold] her gold Ht.   544 vpon erþe]
here T, H9, Hr, *mg.* Hr; here in erþe Rb, P.   546 stench] *add canceled* beþ
war Hr.—þat is helle . . . stench] *om.* Ra; *add* and beþ ware P.—be] *add* sogret
P.   546-547 in stede . . . smellynge] *om.* T; *mg.* Hr; þat no man may suffre
hit P.   547 of soote smellynge] *om.* Rb.—as Ysaye seiþ] *om.* T, Hr; as seiþ
Seynt Jerom and ȝet P.
   *Job xxiiij°] *om.* Hr, U, Hu, H2; *lh.* Ht; *in text* P.
   *Ysaye 3°] *om.* Hu, P; Ysaie *lh.* Ht; Ysaie U.

ʒe be nouʒt wiþ þis pot ne wiþ þe womman þerinne, *and*
on al man*ere* þat ʒe be not weddid to hir*e*, for þanne ʒe
most be boþe oon. þis is þilke fowle lecherous wo*mman*   550

fol. 7ʳᵇ

"þe kyngis *and* þe marchau*n*dis of þe erþe haueþ do le- /
cherie wiþ, *and* of her*e* v*er*tu þey haueþ be maad riche."

*Apocalyp-
sis xviijº.
(3, 8-10,
16-17)

Whos da*m*pnacio*n* is write i*n* þe bok of Pr*i*uytes in þes
wordis: "In oo day shal come alle þe ve*n*geaunces of her*e*:
deþ, wepy*n*ge, *and* hungr*e*, *and* fier shal bre*n*ne hir*e*.   555
For strong is God þat shal ve*n*ge hy*m* on hir*e*. *And* þan
schulleþ wepe *and* weyle vpon hir*e* þe ky*n*gis of þe erþe
þat haueþ do lecherie wi*þ* hyr*e* *and* han lyued in delicis,
wha*n* þey schulleþ see smok of hir*e* bre*n*ny*n*ge sto*n*dynge
afeer, wepy*n*ge, *and* weyly*n*ge, *and* seyinge: Alas, alas   560
þilke gr*e*te citee þat was cloþed wiþ bisse *and* purpr*e*
and brasile, *and* ou*er*gilt wi*þ* gold *and* pr*e*cious stones

C
548 be] *ins. above.*   552 wiþ] *om.*
Var
547-548 þat ʒe be nouʒt wiþ] *om.* Rb.   548 be] wende Ht; go H9, A, H2; deele
U; *om.* Hu; *mg. lh.* have to do S; *blank space* Ra.—ne] *add* deele not U.   549
man*ere*] *add* beþ war for Godes loue P.   550 most] *om.* T, Hr, P.—fowle]
om. Ht.   555-556 deþ . . . And] *om.* Rb.   561 cloþed] arayed P.   562 gold
and] *om.* P; *add* wiþ S, A, H2, U, Hu.
   *Apoc*a*lypsis xviiijº] *in text* P; *om.* Hu, P; *lh.* Reuel. Ht; Apocalypsis U.

and p*er*les. For *in* on hour alle þese gr*e*te richessis
beþ distroied." Þ*an* shulleþ þey seye þat shulleþ be
damned wiþ hir*e:* "We haue erred fro þe wey of trewþe   565
and of ryʒtfulnesse. Liʒt haþ not schyned to vs, *and* þe
su*n*ne of vndirsto*n*dyng haþ not rysen to vs. We haueþ be
maade wery i*n* þe wey of wikkednesse *and* of loost, *and* we
haueþ go harde weyes. But þe wey of God we knewe not.
What haþ p*r*ide p*r*ofited to vs oþ*er* þe bost of our*e* richesse?   570
What haþ it brouʒt to vs? Al is go as a schadewe of deeþ,
and we mowe now schewe no tokene of holynesse; in our*e*
wikkednesse we beþ wasted awey."

Þynk þerfore, I rede, þat þou schalt ʒelde r*e*kenyng
of þy balye.   575

Her*e* endiþ þe first p*ar*tie of þis sermou*n*.

C
570 bost] book.   576 first] *ins. above.*
Var
570 bost] book Ra, A, H2, U, Hu, S.—our*e*] *om.* T, H9, Hr, P.   571-572 What
. . . *and*] *om.* Rb.   574 I rede] nowe be tyme Rb; *add* bi tyme H9.—þat] how
T, Hr, P.—ʒelde] ʒyue P.   576 Here . . . sermou*n*] *om.* Rb.
    *Sapi*en*tia* 8°] *om.* Ht, Ra, U, Hu, P; Sapientia 5 H2, S, Rb, *lh.* A; Sapientia
5 aut 8 H9; Apoc. 5 Hr.

*Sapien-
tia* 8°.
(v. 6-13)

fol. 7ᵛᵃ   / Here bygynneþ þe secunde part.

In þis secunde partie, þurgh þe helpe of God, I wole
schewe first who shal clepe vs to þis rekenyng, aftirwar
byfore what iuge we shulleþ rekene, *and* last what puny-   580
schynge shal be do to hem þat ben fonden false seruauntis
and wickid *and* what reward schal be ʒeue to hem þat ben
founden goode *and* trewe.

For þe firste ʒe shal wyten þat þer shullen be tweye
domes: þe firste anoon aftir þe departyng of þe body   585
and þe soule, *and* þis shal be special, *and* of þis reke-
*Lucam   nynge oþer doom spekeþ þe gospel of Luk; þe secunde re-
xvjᵒ   kenynge oþer dom shal be anoon aftir þe general resurreccion, *and* þat shal be vniuersal, *and* of þis it is spoke
*Matthaeum in þe gospel of Matheu. To þe first eueriche man shal   590
xxvᵒ. (31-   be cleped aftir oþer, as þe world passiþ; to þe secunde
46)   alle schulle come togidere in þe strook of an eiʒe.

C
577 *upper mg.* 7ᵛᵃ. 578 þe] *om.*
Var
577 Here] and now Ht, Ra, S, A, U, Hu; *om.* T, Hr, P.—Here . . . part] *om.*
Rb, H9.—part] *om.* A, H2. 578 þis] whiche T, H9, Hr, P.—þurgh] bi A,
H2. 582 be ʒeue] come H9. 584 For . . . wyten] *om.* Rb.—wyten] vndir-
stondyn Ht. 585 firste] *add* dome T, Hr, H9, P. 586-587 of þis . . . Luk] *om.*
H9, P.—rekenynge oþer] *om.* P. 587 oþer doom] *om.* Ht.—þe secunde] and
anoþir H9. 587-590 þe gospel . . . spoke in] *om.* T.—þe secunde . . . Matheu]
mg. Hr. 588 anoon aftir] *om.* P.—general] *add* at þe wordles ende whenne
alle men and wymmen shal ʒyue reknynge of al her lyuynge in þis worlde P.
588-589 resurreccion . . . vniuersal] *om.* P. 589 þis] *add* reknyng or dome P.
590-592 To þe first . . . an eiʒe] *om.* A, H2. 592 strook] twynkelyng Ra, T,
Hr, H9, P; sterynge Rb.
    *Lucam xvjᵒ] *om.* C, Ht, Ra, S, T, A, H2, H9, Hr, P, Hu; Lucam 3 Rb.
    *Matthaeum xxvᵒ] *om.* Hu; *lh.* Matthaeum Ht; *in text* P.

To þe first men schulleþ be clepid wiþ þre somoners
oþer seryauntis: þe firste is sekenesse; þe secunde is
elde; *and* þe þridde is deþ. Þe first warneþ; þe secunde   595
þreteneþ; *and* þe þridde takiþ. Þis is a cundelich ordre,
but oþer wile it fallyt vnkyndelich. For summe we seeþ
fol. 7ᵛᵇ dye þat wisten neuere / what was sekenesse ne elde, as
childeren þat beþ sodenly slayn. *And* summe, ȝe þe most
part, þat dieþ nowadayes dieþ bifore here kynde age of   600
deþ.

Þerfore y seye þat þe first þat clepeþ to þis special
rekenynge is sekenesse. *And* þis is double: for sum is
sekenesse þat folwiþ al mankynde, so þat euery man haþ it;
and sum is sikenesse þat sum men haueþ, but not alle. Ȝit
þe first sekenesse is double, for sum is wiþinne in þe   605
myȝttes of þe soule, *and* sum is wiþouten in feblenesse
of þe body, þat nedis most be distroied on wham tyme by
hymself is cause of corrupcion, as þe philosofre seiþ.

Þat þere be feblenesse *and* sekenesse may we see herby:

C
594 oþer] oure.   600 of] *add* þe.   608 corrupcion] corrūpcion.—þe] *ins.*
above.
Var
593 *add mg.* nota tres apparitoreþ Hr.   596-597 Þis is a . . . vnkyndelich]
om. Ht.   597 vnkyndelich] *om.* Rb, S, A, H2, U, Hu; *marked out* Hr.—
summe] *add* men Ht.—we seeþ] *om.* Rb.   599 ȝe] we seyþ T, Hr, P.   600 nowadayes dieþ] *om.* T, Hr, H9, P.   602 y seye þat] *om.* Rb, U.—Þerfore] for A,
H2; As for U.—special] *om.* Ht, Rb.   603-604 *And* þis . . . sekenesse] *om.* S.
602-605 for sum . . . double] *om.* Rb.   604 haueþ] *add* it A, H2.—ȝit] *add* I
seye T, Hr, P.   605 wiþinne] sicknes in T, P; seke wiþinne Rb.   606 is] haþ
sekenes Rb.—feblenesse] sicknes T, P.   607-608 on wham . . . as] *om.* Rb.
609 be] *add* many diuerse T, Hr, P.—sekenesse] *add* and þat we mowe knowe
and Rb.—see] *add* wel Ht, Rb, A, Hu.—herby] *om.* Hu.—may we see herby]
om. T, P.

þat þouȝ a man schutte out of þe hous of his herte al maner   610
of worldly and fleschly þouȝtis, ȝit vnneþe schal a man
for out þat he can do, þenke on God only þe space of a
Pater Noster þat sum oþer þouȝt of þyng þat is passynge
entriþ into þe soule and drawiþ hire fro þat contempla-
cion. But O Lord God, what sekenesse is þis and heuy   615
birdene vpon þe sones of Adam þat on þe foule muk and fen
of þe world we mowe þynke long ynow, but vpon þat þat
þe soule shulde most delectacion haue by kynde mowe we

fol. 8ra   not / þynke only so litle a space but ȝif þe kokkil entre
among þe whete. Of þis sekenesse spak Poule whan he seide   620

*Romanos
vijᵒ. (23)   "I se a lawe in my lymes fyȝttynge aȝenis þe lawe of my
spirit and takynge me into þe lawe of synne." So þat
it fareþ by vs as by a man þat wolde loke stedefastly
aȝens þe sunne and may not do it longe for noþyng. And
certis þat is for no defaute þat is in þe sunne, for sche   625
is most cler in herself, and so bi resoun best shulde be
yseye; but it is for feblenesse of þe mannes eyȝe. Ryȝt

C
611 and] an. 616 on þe] *om.* 624 not] *om.* 627 it] *ins. above.*
Var
out—hole in MS 624-625 þyng . . . þat; 625-626 for . . . most; 626-627
shulde . . . but] H2. 610 þe hous of] *om.* T, Hr, P.—maner] *om.* T, Hr, P.
611 þouȝtis] lustis T, P.—a man] he Ht. 613 oþer] *om.* P.—þouȝt of] *om.* T,
H9, P. 616 sones] sowles Rb.—fen] filthe Rb, P. 617 þat þat] þee þat Ra,
S, H9, H2, A; þyne P; thinge Rb. 620 whan he seide] *om.* P. 622 þe lawe of]
om. A. H2. 623 as] *add* it doþe Ht; *add* it fareþ P.—stedefastly] *om.* H9.
626 in herself] *om.* Ht; in her shewyng T, Hr, P. 627 Ryȝt] syȝt Ht.
   *Romanos vijᵒ] *om.* C, Ht, Ra, T, A, H2, Hr, Hu; *in text* P; *lh.* S.

so siþ Adam, oure first fadre, was put out of paradis, al
his ospryng haþ be þus sek. As þe prophte seiþ: "Oure

Ezechiel xviij. (2)   fadres haueþ bite a bytter grape, *and* þe teeþ of þe   630
children ben woxe on egge.

þe secunde sekenesse, þat is comune to al mankynde,
comeþ of feblenesse of þe body: as hungre *and* þrust,
cold *and* hete, sorwe *and* werynesse, *and* many oþere. As

Job xviij. (xiv. 1)   Job seiþ: "A man þat is borne of a womman, lyuynge a   635
litle wile, is fulfillid wiþ many myseses. But þer
is oþer siknesses þat comeþ to sum men, but not to alle,
as lepre, palesie, feuere, *and* dropesie, *and* blyndnesse,
and manye oþere. As it was seid to þe puple of Israel

Deuterono- mium xxviij. (58-59)   in holy writ: "But ȝif þou kepe þe mawdementis þat beþ   640
wryten on þis book, God schal eken þe sekenesse of þe
and of þy seed, grete sekenesses *and* abidynge, worst

fol. 8rb   / *and* euerelastynge.

And ȝe shulle vndirstonde þat God sendiþ oþer-wile

C

632 al] alle *with* le *marked for erasure.*
Var

629 Oure] hour S; ȝoure A, H2. 630 bite] etyn Ht, S, A, Hr, U, Hu, H2.
632 þat is comune] *om.* T, Hr, P. 634 werynesse] wrecchidnesse T, Hr, P.—
oþere] *om.* H9. 635-636 A man . . . myseses] *om.* Ht. 636 myseses] disesis
H9; wrecchidnesses A, H2, Hu; meschiefs U. 641 þe] grett Rb; þin T; þi A,
Hr, 641-642 of þe . . . sekenesses] *om.* A, H2; and þe seckness of kynde þat
is T, Hr, P. 642 abidynge] *add* and þat is T, Hr, P. 644 vndirstonde] answere Ht.

   *Ezechiel xviij] *om.* H9, P; Osee 18 Hr, T, Hu, *lh.* Ht.
   *Job xviij] *in text* P; *om.* Hu; Job U, *lh.* Ht; Job 14 H9; Job 13 A, H2.
   *Deuteronomium xxviij] *om.* U, Hu, Ht; *in text* P.

suche sekenesse to goode men *and* oþer-wile to schrewis.   645
To goode men God doþ it for two causis, *and* þat is soþ
of sykenesse I wole to be vnderstonde also of alle maner
tribulacion.

   Þe first cause: for þey shulden euere knowe þat
þey haueþ no perfeccion of hemself but of God only, *and*   650
to ekene here mekenesse. *And* þus seiþ Poule: "Lest þe
gretnesse of reuelaciouns rere me vp into pride, me is
ȝiue a prikke of my flesch, þe angel of Sathanas to smyte
me on þe necke. Wherfore y haue þryþes prayed God þat
he schulde go fro me; *and* He answerede me, 'My grace   655
is sufficiaunt to þe, for vertu is fulfillid in sykenesse.' "
Wheron þus seiþ þe glose: þe fend, askyng Job to be temptid,
was herd of God, *and* nouȝt þe apostle axinge his temptacion to be remowid. God herde hym þat schulde be dampned,
and he herde not hym þat he wolde saue. For ofte þe seke   660
man axkiþ many þyngis of þe leche þat he wole not ȝyue
hym, *and* þat is for to make hym hool of his sykenesse.

*II Corin-
thios xij.
(7-9)

C
650 þey] *mg.*   660 *and*] *add* so.
Var
646 is soþ] es to say S; I seie Ht, Hu; is seid Ra, Rb, U; *om.* T, Hr, P.   647 I
wole] ȝe schul T, Hr, P.   651 ekene] multiplie Rb.—mekenesse] *mg. lh.* S.—
seiþ] *add* Seynt H9, H2.—Poule] *add* ne magnitude revelationun P, *mg.* Hr.
653 flesch] selfe Rb.   657 fend] *om.* Ht.   660 herde] *om.* Rb.   662 sykenesse]
add and þat is for he wole make him hole of his sykenes Hr.
   *II Corinthios xij] *om.* T, Hr, Hu, P; Paul *lh.* Ht; Cor . . . xii H2.

Also God sendiþ seyntis often sykenesse *and* persecucion to ȝyue vs senful wrecchis ensaumple of pacience.

fol. 8ᵛᵃ For / ȝif he suffre his seyntis to haue suche tribula-   665
cion in þis world *and* þey þankyn hym þerof, moche more
wrechis, þat God sendiþ to nouȝt þe hondrid parte of here
sorwe, shulde bere it mekely, siþ we haue disserued a
þousand so moche as þey haueþ. Wherfore of Tobie, þat an
a day whan he was wery of buryenge of pore men, þe whiche   670

*Tobi ijº
capitulo.*
(10-14) schulde haue leyen vnbiried *and* han ben etyn of houndis
and foulis as carienes of oþere vnresonable bestis, "whan
for werynesse he had leid hym to reste, *and* þourh Goddis
sufferaunce þe swalwes þat bredden aboue on his hous
maden ordure into his eiȝen, *and* he wexe blynd," þus   675
it is write: "þis temptacion forsoþe, þerfore, God
suffride to come to hym þat to hem þat comen aftir
schulde be ȝeue ensaumple of pacience, as by þe temptacion of holy Job. For siþ fro his childehod euermore
he dredde God, *and* euere kepte his hestis, he was not   680

C
676 þerfore] *om.*
Var
out 666 hym . . . moche; 667 to . . . parte] *hole in MS.* H2.
out 668-680 mekely . . . was not H2.
663 often] *add* tyme T, Hr, P; *add* tymes Rb. 663-665 often . . . seyntis] *om.*
H9. 665 haue] suffre T, Hr. 666 more] *add* we Ra, A, H2, U, Hu. 667 of
here so myche P; of owre A, H2. 669 þousand] hundred Hu.—Wherfore]
add we reden Ht, Ra, Hr, T, P, H9; *add* see U. 671 leyen] ben Ht, Rb. 672
vnresonable] *om.* Rb; vnskilful A. 675-676 þus it is write] *om.* H9; *add* of him
T, Hr, P. 676 þerfore] *om.* Rb, U, P. 677-678 þat to hem . . . schulde] of his
aftercomers P. 678-679 temptacion] ensample T, Hr, P. 679 Job] Thobie
U.—siþ] *add* þe tyme of Rb. 680 hestis] commaundementis Rb, P.
   Tobi ijº capitulo] om. T, Hr, Hu, P, Ht, Rb, H9, A, U.

agreued aȝens God þat þe myscheues blyndenesse fel to
hym, but vnmouable dwellide in þe drede of God, þankyng
hym alle þe dayes of his lif." Lo þat holy writ seiþ
expressely þat God suffrede þis holy man to haue þis sykenesse to ȝeue hem þat shulden comen aftir hym ensauple   685
of pacience.

fol. 8ᵛᵇ   Also oþerwile God / sendiþ siknesse *and* tribulacion
to wickid men, *and* þat for two causis. First, for þey
schulde þe raþere drede God *and* leue here synne. As it
*ii P*salmo*   is writen: "Þer siknesse haueþ be multiplied, *and* aftir   690
(xv. 4)   þey haue hiȝed to Godward." For we seeþ ofte men in
sekenesse knowe here God þat neuere wolden haue turned
to hym while þey hadden ben hoole. Also God sendiþ hem
syknesse ofte to agaste oþer men leste þey folweden
*ijᵒ Macha-   here synnes. As þe sekenesse of Antioche, whom "God   695
baeorum
74ᵒ (ix.   smot wiþ suche a sekenesse þat wermes skatered out of his
9-18)   body while he lyuede—in so ferforþ þat he stank so

C
688 þat for] on
Var
out H2.
681 myscheues] suche P. 682 but] *add* stedfastly and P.—vnmouable] couen-
able Hu. 685 þat shulden comen aftir hym] *om.* Rb. 689 schulde] *om.* A.
689-690 As it is writen] as þe prophete seys in þe sawtur boke, Psalmo 15 Rb;
add in þe sauter H9; *add* here T; *add* in þe psalme þus P. 690-691 Þer siknesse
. . . Godward] *om.* Ht. 692-693 þat neuere . . . ben] knowe hym in Rb.
692 turned] *add* to Godward T, Hr, P. 694 agaste] fere Rb; chastise P.—
foleweden sȝolde dwelle in T, P. 695 of] *add* Kyng H9.—Antioche] *add* þe
kyng P. 697 þat he stank so] *om.* Ra.

    *ii P*salmo*] *om.* Ht, Ra, T, Hu, P; iij Psalmo S; Psalmo 15 H9, U; in Psalmo
Hr; *lh.* Psalmo 15, v. 3 A.

    *ijᵒ Machabaeorum 74ᵒ] *om.* Ht, T, Hr, Hu; 2ᵒ Machabaeorum 9 Ra, S, H9,
A; Machabaeorum vjᵒ cᵒ U; *in text* Machab. 9 P.

foule þat he was heuy þerwiþ *and* myȝt not suffre it, *and*
at þe laste þ*at* he ne myȝt nouȝt hymself suffr*e* his owne
stynch. *And* þ*an* he gan to knowe hymself *and* seyde, 'It is   700
ryȝtful to be suget to God, *and* a dedly man nouȝt to holde
hy*m*self euene to God.' " *And* þe story seiþ þ*at* "he axkid
mercy of God, of whom he shulde no m*er*cy haue, *and* made a
uow to God: þat he schulde make þe citee of Ier*usalem*
free, *and* þe Iewes to make he*m* as free as me*n* of Athenis;   705

fol. 9ʳᵃ   *and* þat / he wolde honour*e* Goddis te*m*ple wiþ *precio*u*ns*
aray, *and* multiplie þe holy vesselis, *and* fynde of his
owne rente cost *and* spensis p*er*tiny*n*ge to þe sacrifise;
and he wolde bycome a Iew, *and* go ou*er* al þe lond, *and*
*pr*eche Goddis myȝt. *And* ȝit God ȝaf hy*m* no mercy." *And*   710
I trowe certeyn þat þat was for he axkid it to late.
What mede was it to him to forsake his wickidnesse whan

C
708 sacrifise] sacrise.   712 him to] *ins. above.*
Var
out H2.
698 foule . . . suffre it] *om.* Ra.—he was] his frendis were Ht, U, *mg.* Hr; is
men Rb; his owne men were A; alle hise werene S; hise werun Hu; he hymself
was T, H9, P.—*and* myȝt] þat þei myȝt Ht, *mg.* Hr.   699 at þe laste] *om.* Hr.—
hymself *om.* Ht.   700 knowe] God and Rb.   701 nouȝt] *om.* Rb.   703 of
whom he shulde no m*er*cy haue] *om.* T, H9, P; *mg.* Hr.   705 make] take T,
Hr, P.—me*n*] *om.* Ht.—Athenis] *add* þe wiche a lytyll before he had cast to
haue fordon and to haue ȝeuen þe bodyes of hem to fowles and to wilde beestes
and seid Rb.   706-707 wiþ *precio*u*ns aray] wiþ grett areye and preciose Rb.
710 mercy] suche mercy as he desyred T, Hr, H9, P.   711 was] *add* oþer for
God weste þat he wold noȝt aftirward haue holde couenaunt of þis oþer T,
Hr, P; *add* eiþer good to seie þat he wolde not aftirward haue holde couenaunt
eiþir H9.—for he axkid it] *om.* Rb.—*add lower mg.* þe cursid kyng antiok
preied þe lord, of whom he hadde not mercy; for þe wordis whiche he preiede
and seyde weren seid in dispensynge of hymself H9.

he was vnmyȝti to do good oþer euel? *And* by þys vengeance
þat God tok of þis kyng shulde me*n* see what it is to be
vnobedient to God. *And* also it is to take hede þat whan   715
so eu*er*e sekenesse comeþ, eu*er*e it scheweþ þat he þat
suffreþ is dedly *and* þat he schal nede dye. For þowȝ
he may skape his siknesse, ȝit may he not skape þe deþ.
And so þou most nedis come to þy rekeny*n*ge.

   þe secu*n*de somner þat schal clepe þe to þis p*ar*ti-   720
culer dom is elde. *And* þe co*n*dici*on* of þis is þis: þat
þouȝ he tarie wiþ þe, he wole not leue þe til he bry*n*ge
þe to þe þridde, þat is deeþ.

   But þer be many þat þouȝ þey haue þis somenour wiþ
he*m*, þey taken none hede. He seeþ his hed hory, his bak   725
crokeþ, his breþ sty*n*keþ, his teeþ falleþ, his eiȝen
derkeþ, his visage reueliþ, his eren wexeþ heuy to her*e*.
What meneþ al þis but þat elde som*m*ouneþ þe to þe dom?
fol. 9ʳᵇ But / what more madhede may be þa*n* a man be clepid *and*

C
715 to take] *om.* to.
Var
out H2.
713 euel] *add* naþeles I trowe þat he was noȝt dampned siþþe he had suche
repentaunce, for Repentaunce in þis lif comyþ neuer to late if it be trewe T,
Hr, H9, P; *add mg. lh.* Neuerthelesser I knowe he was not damned in as much
as he had such repentauns, for repenaunce in this lyfe comith neuer to late if
it be true S.   713-714 þys vengeance þat God tok of] *om.* Rb.   714 me*n*] *add*
þat will take grace take ensampull Rb.   716 sekenesse comeþ] *mg. lh.* S.—he]
þe man Rb.   716-717 þat suffreþ] *om.* Rb.   719 þy rekeny*n*ge] ȝelde rekenyng
of þin bayly T, Hr, H9, P.   725 He] this somenour P.   727 visage] face Ht.—
here] *add* his hondes quaken and many oþur tokons vnlustie to þe vorld and
to his own frendis Rb, H9.   728 What . . . dom] *om.* A.

drawe to so dredful a rekeny*n*ge þere, but he answer*e*   730
wel þer*e*? He forfeteþ boþe body *and* soule to da*m*nacio*n*
foreu*ere*, ʒif he, seeynge a litle myrþe on þe weye, þinke
so mochel þeronne þat he forʒetiþ who draweþ hym oþ*er*
whedir he draweþ hym. So doþ he þat is smyten wiþ age,
and lykeþ so on þe false worldlis welþe þat he forʒetiþ   735
whodir he is aweye.

*Augustinus
de xij
abusionibus Herfore seiþ þe holy docto*ur*: þat among alle þe
abusiones of þe world, most is a olde ma*n* þat is obstinat.
For he þynkiþ not on his owʒt goynge of þis world, ne of
his passyng i*n*to þe lyf þat is to come. He heereþ massan-   740
ger*e*s of deþ, *and* he leeueþ he*m* nouʒt. *And* þe cause is
þis: for þe þrefold cord þat suche an old ma*n* is bou*n*de
wiþ is hard to breke. þis cord is custom, þat is of þre
plytis: þat is of ydel þouʒt, vnhonest speche, *and* wickid

Var
out H2.
730 rekenynge] *add* þat he may vnneþ skape itt Rb.—he] *add* ʒelde resonabull
Rb. 731 to] *add* euerlastynge Rb. 732 foreu*ere*] *om.* Rb; *add* what is more
folys þan Rb.—seeynge] *add* by þe way Rb.—litle] *add* veyn worldlych T, Hr,
H9, P. 732-733 on þe weye . . . þat he] *om.* Rb. 734 whedir he draweþ hym]
and where to and whatt perels folowyn Rb.—draweþ hym] is somonned H9,
T, Hr, P.—smyten] drawen Rb.—age] *add* toward his dome þat comes with is
dethe Rb. 735 *and* lykeþ] and þenkes Rb.—so] *add* muche Rb, U.—welþe]
add as lordshipe purchasyng, richesse, children, or ony worldli þing H9, Rb.
736 aweye] *add* and so nyʒ is dome Rb, H9. 737 þe holy] *om.* P.—docto*ur*]
add de Lyra P. 738-740 most is . . . passyng] *om.* H9. 739 of þis world] *om.*
Rb. 739-740 ne of . . . to come] *om.* T, Hr, P. 741 leeueþ] troweþ P.
744 ydel] euel A.—*and*] *add* þe þridde is P.
    *Augustinus de xij abusionibus] *om.* C, Ht, Ra, Rb, S, H9, A, Hu; doctor
de lyra T, Hr, *in text* P.

dede—þe whiche ȝif þey growe wiþ a man fro þe childhod   745
into mannes age, þey make a treble corde to bynde þe olde

*Ysaye
viijº.
(lviii. 6)*

man in custom of synne. Herfore seiþ Ysaye? "Breke þe
bondes of synne." Þynke, herfore, who so euere þat þou be
þat art þus somened, þat þou myȝt not skape þat þou ne
schalt ȝelde rekenynge of þy bailye.   750

Þe þridde somenour to þis rekenyng is deþ, *and* þe
condicion of þis is þis: þat whanne so euere he comeþ—
first, oþer secunde, oþer last—he ne spareþ neyþer

fol. 9va

powere, ne ȝougþe; / ne he dredeþ no þretyng, ne takiþ
hede of no praiere ne of no ȝifte; ne he graunteþ no   755
respit; but wiþouten dalay he bryngeþ forþ to þe dom.

*Augustinus.
Hesichio
epistola
80ª*

Herfor seiþ Seynt Austyn: "Wel auȝte euery man
drede þe day of his deeþ; for in what state so euere a
mannes laste day fyndeþ hym whan he goþ out of þis world,

C
754 ne he] *add* ne. 755 ne he] *add* ne.
Var
out H2.
745 þe childhod] ȝounge Rb. 746 treble] þrefolde Ht, Rb.—bynde] blynde
Ra; brynge U. 747 seiþ] *add* þe prophete Hr. 753 first . . . last] in ȝouþ or
in age Rb. 754 powere, ne ȝougþe] pore ne ryche, olde ne ȝonge Ht, Rb, A;
poyr ne ȝonge T; pore ne ryche Hr; *add mg.* age ne ȝougþe, fayre ne foule Hr;
add kynge ne knaue Rb. 756 wiþouten] *add* any U, T, Hr, H9, P.
   *Ysaye viijº *in text* P; *om.* Hu; Ysaye lviij S, Rb, A, U; viij T; Ysaye 8 al 58
H9; c. 56 Ht.
   Augustinus . . . .] lh. lower mg. H9; *om. in all other MSS.*

in þe same state he bryngeþ hym to his dom." Herfore   760
seiþ þe wyse man: Sone, þenk on þy laste end, *and* þou
schalt neu*ere* synne. Þ*erfore*, y rede, þenk þat þou schalt
ȝelde rekeny*n*ge of þy bailie.

    I seyde also þat þ*er* schulde be anoþ*er* dom to þe whiche
alle me*n* schulle*n* come togyder*e*, *and* þis schal be vniu*er*sel.   765
And riȝt as to þat oþ*er* dom eu*er*y ma*n* schal be clepid wiþ
þr*e* somenoures, so to þis dom al þis world schal be clepid
wiþ þr*e* gen*er*al cleperis. *And* riȝt as þe oþ*ere* þre messageþ
a ma*n*nes ende, so þese telleþ þe ende of þe world. Þe firste
is þe worldlis sykenesse; þe secu*n*de is feblenesse; *and*   770
þe þridde is his ende. And þe sekenesse of þe world þou
schalt knowe by charites acoldyng; his elde *and* his feblenesse þou schalt knowe by tokenes fulfillynge; *and* his
ende þou schalt knowe by Ante*cristis* pursuynge.

    First y seye þou schalt knowe þe worldis sykenesse   775

C
761 man] *om.*—end] *om.*
Var
out 760-774 in þe same ... Ante*cristis* H2. 764-775 T, Hr, P.
761 wyse man] sapiens Rb; *add* Salomon P.—man] *om.* S, Ra.—laste end] day
of deþ T, Hr.—end] *om.* U, Rb; day A, H9, P. 762 synne] deye U.—þ*erfore*,
y rede] and þus þou haste grett cause to Rb. 765-766 be uniu*er*sel ... man
schal] *om.* S. 767 somenoures] *add* oþur sariaundes Rb.—clepid] called Rb.
768 riȝt] *om.* Rb, A.—messageþ] messageris tellen H9; *add lh. mg.* tell S.
769 firste] *add* clepere H9. 769-770 firste is þe] *lh. mg.* Hu. 770 secunde] *add*
clepere H9.

by charites acoldynge. Clerkes þat treteþ of kyndis seiþ

fol. 9vb þat a body / is sik whan his kyndely heete is to lytle
or whanne is vnkendely heete is to moche. Siþ þan al
mankynde is oo body whos kyndely heete is charite, þat is
loue to oure God *and* to oure neyȝebore, vnkyndely heete is   780
lustful loue to oþre creatures. Whan þerfore þou seest
þat þe loue of men to Godward *and* to here neiȝebores is
litle *and* feynt *and* þe loue to worldly þyngis *and* to lustes
of þe flesch is gret *and* feruent, þanne wite þou wel þat
vnkyndely hete is to gret *and* kyndely heete is to lytle.   785
    þat þis be a knoweleche of þis siknesse may I *pr*eue

*Matthaeum
xxiiij.
(12) by auctorite of C*r*ist; for he hymself ȝaf hem as a sygne
of þe drawynge to þe ende of þe world "for þat wickednesse

*ij can*oni-
ca Joannem
ij ca*pitulo*.
(17) schal be in plente, charite schal acolde." Þe*r*fore wha*n*ne
þou seest charite þus litle in þe world *and* wickednesse   790
encr*e*sse, knowe wel "þat þis world passiþ *and* his welþe,"

C
776 *add mg.* n*ota.*   778 vnkendely] kendely.—þan] *ins. above.*
Var
out T, P, Hr.   788-791 þe world . . . welþe H2.
777 kyndely] bodily A, H2.   778 heete is] *om.* A, H2.   779 kyndely] *om.* Ht.
780 neyȝebore] euene crystyn Ht.   787 sygne] figure U, Hu.   788 world] *add*
in þe gospell seyinge Rb, H9.—wickednesse] siknesse S; *lh. mg.* S.   789
charite] *add* of monye Hu.—schal] *add* waxe A, Rb.
    Matthaeum xxiiij] *om.* Ra, U, Hu; *lh.* A; *lh.* Matthaeum 23 Ht; *lh. add*
quoniam abundabit iniquitas et refrigescet charitas multorum H9.
    *ij can*onica Joannem ij ca*pitulo*] *om.* Ht, Ra, Rb, T, H9, A, Hr, U, Hu.

and þat þis somenour is come. *And* þus seiþ Seynt Poule:

*II Timo-
theum iij.
(1-5)* "Wite þou wel þat in þe last dayes schal come perilous
tymes. *And* þere schulleþ be men lowyng hemself, þat is
to seye here bodies, coueytous by pride, vnobedient to   795
fadre *and* modre; vnkynde felowes wiþouten affeccion, wiþouten pees; blameres, vncontinent, vnmylde, wiþouten be-
nignite; traytoures, rebel; swellynge loueres of lustes

fol. 10ʳᵃ mo / re þan of God, hauynge a liknesse of pite, *and* deny-
enge þe ventu þerof." *And* þes flee. Whan þou seest þe pe-   800
ple byside on suche condiciones, wite wel þat þe first
somenour warneþ al þe world þat þe day of rekenynge draweþ
toward.

   Þe secunde somenour þat warneþ al þe world is elde
of þe world *and* his feblenesse. *And* þis schewiþ tokenes   805
*Actus
1º. (7)* fulfillyng, but y knowe wel þat we "be not sufficiaunt to
knowe þe tymes oþer þe whyles, þat þe Fadre in Trinite
haþ putte in his owne power" to schewe certeynly þe day,

Var
out T, Hr, P, H2.
793 þe] owre A.   794-795 þat is to seye here bodies] *om.* Ht.   796 felowes]
wicked A.   797 blameres] backitours Rb.—vncontinent, vnmylde] *om.* Rb;
vnchast A.   798-799 swellynge . . . of God] *om.* Ht.   805-806 *and* his feblenesse . . . fulfillyng] *om.* Ht.   807 þe tymes] þe certeynte of tymes Rb.—oþer þe
whyles] *om.* Ht, Rb.—Trinite] heven Rb.
   *II Timotheum iij] *om.* C, Ra, S, T, Hr, Hu; *lh.* Ht; Paulus 2 Rb.
   *Actus 1º] *om.* Ht, Ra, Rb, T, H9, Hr, A, U, Hu.

ȝer, oþer hour of þis dom, siþ þis knowleche was hid fro
þe priue aposteles of Crist *and* also fro Cristis manhod,   810
as to schewe it to vs. Naþeles we moweþ by auctorite of
holy writ, wiþ resoundes *and* exposiciones of seyntis, wel
and openly schewe þat þis day of wreche is nyȝe.

But ȝit lest any man seye in his herte, as it is
write of folye baileues, þat þey schal seye: "My lord   815
þat is tarieþ to come to þe dom, *and* vpon hope herof he
take to smyte seruantis *and* hynen of God, ette *and* drynke
and make hym drunke," I schal schewe þat þis day is at þe
hond. How nyȝe, neþeles, can y not seye, ne wole; for ȝif
Poule seyde, now for a þousand ȝeer *and* þre hundryd *and* mo   820
passid, / we ben þilke "into whom þe endes of þe world beþ
come," moche raþere mowe we seye þe same þat beoþ so moche
nerre þe ende þan he was.

Also Seynt Johan Crisostom seiþ: "þou seest oueral
derkenesses, *and* þou douȝtist þat þe day is go. First on   825
þe valeyes is derkenessis, whan þe day drawiþ donward.

Side notes:
*Lucam xijᵒ. (45)
*I Corinthios x. (11) fol. 10ʳᵇ
*Crisostomus, Omelia 25. Operis Imperfecti

C
817 drynke] drynge.   821 endes] s *ins. above.*
Var
out T, Hr, P.   809-814 ȝer, . . . seye in his H2.
809 oþer hour] *om.* Ht.   810 Crist] *add* from angels of heven Rb.   811 as to
schewe it to vs] *om.* Ht.   814-815 as it is write] *om.* U.   816 hope] *om.* A, H2.
—herof] *om.* H2.   817 God] *add* and þei A, H2; *add* he Rb.—and drynke] *om.*
A, H2.   818 and make hym drunke] with dronkon men Rb.—schewe] *add*
wiþ Goddis helpe Ht.   819 ne wole] *om.* Rb.   821 passid] *om.* Rb.   822-824
beoþ . . . Seynt] *om.* U.   824 Seynt Johan] *om.* Ht.—Johan] *om.* S; J Ht.
826 drawiþ] bowiþ H2.
    *Lucam xijᵒ] *om.* Ra, T, Hr, U, Hu, H2; *lh.* Lucam 22 Ht.
    *I Corinthios x] *om.* C, Ht, Ra, Rb, T, H9, Hr, A, Hu, H2.
    *Crisostomus . . .] *om.* Hu, T, Hr; Cris, omelia 26 op. imp. Rb, S, H9; Cris.
op. imp. Omelia 12 A; Crisostomus Ht, Ra, U; *om.* H2.

Whan þerfore þou seest þe valeis is derkid, why doutist
þou wheþer it be neiȝ euen. But ȝif þou see þe sunne so
lowe þat derkenesse is vpon þe hillis, þou wolt seye douteles
þat it is nyȝt. Ryȝt so, ȝif þou see first in þe seculeres   830
and lewede Cristene men bygynne dirkenessis of synnes to
haue þe maystrie, it is tokene þat þis world endiþ. But
whan þou seest prestes, þat beþ put on þe hiȝe coppe of
spiritual dignites, þat schulde be as hilles aboue þe
comune peple in parfit lyuynge, þat dirkenesse of synnes   835
haþ take hem, who douteþ þat þe world nis at þe ende?''

Abbas Joachym   Also Abot Joachym in exposicion of Jeremye seyþ:
Fro þe ȝeer of oure Lord a þousand *and* two hundred, alle
tymes beþ suspecte to me, *and* we be passid on þis suspect
tyme neiȝ two hundrid ȝeer.   840

Hildegare   Also mayde Hildegare in þe book of hyre prophecie
þe þridde partye, þe eleuenþe visioun, þe seuenþe chapitre,
fol. 10ᵛᵃ   meueþ þis resoun: "Ryȝt / as on þe seuenþe day God maad
þe world, so in þe seuene þousand ȝeer þe world schal

C
830 first in] *om.* in.
Var
out T, Hr, P.   828-844 it be neiȝ . . . world schal H2.
827 þerfore] *om.* H2.   827-828 þerfore . . . euen] *om.* Rb.   829 derkenesse
. . . douteles] þe hilles vaxen derke who dowtiþ but þat Rb.   830 Ryȝt so] *add*
seis þis seynt Rb, H9.—first in þe] *om.* Ht, Ra; first þe Rb, S, H9, Hu.   831-832
to haue þe maystrie] *om.* Rb.   833 prestes] *om.* Ht.—coppe] *om.* H9.   838-840
alle . . . ȝeer] *om.* Ht.   841 mayde] *om.* U; *mg. lh.* Hu.   842 þe þridde partye]
om. Hu.
   *Abbas Joachym] *om.* Hu, T, Hr, A, H9; *lh.* J Ht.
   *Hildegare] *om.* Hu, T, Hr.

passe. *And* ryʒt as in þe sixte day man was maad *and* formed,   845
ryʒt so in þe sixe þousand of ʒeris he was bout aʒen *and*
reformed. *And* as in þe seuenþe day þe world was ful maad
and God restede of his worchynge, ryʒt so in þe seuenþe
þousand of ʒeris þe noumbre of hem þat shullen be saued
shal be fulfillid, *and* reste schal be to seyntis ful in   850
body *and* in sowle."

ʒif þan it be so as it semeþ to folewe of þis maidenes
wordis þat seuene þousand of ʒeeris in passynge of þe world
acordiþ to seuene dayes makynge, lat see what lackiþ þat
þis seuene þousand ʒeeris ne be fulfillid. For ʒif we   855
eke þe noumbre of ʒeeris fro þe natyuite of Crist to þe
ʒeeris fro þe bygynnyge of þe world to Crist, *and* þou wolt
folewe Austyn, Bede, and Orosye, *and* most probabyle doctoures tretynge of þis matere, passiþ now almost sexe
þousand *and* sexe hundred, as it is open in a book þat is   860
clepid Speculum Iudiciale. So it sweþ þat þis last day
is more þan half agoo, ʒif we shulde ʒeue credence to
þis maydenes / resoune.

But ʒif wee schul leeue to þe gospel, þanne we schal

fol. 10ᵛᵇ

C
861 So] for.
Var
out T, Hr, P, H2.
845 *and* formed] *om.* Ht.   846-847 ryʒt so . . . reformed] *om.* H9.—*and* re-
formed] *om.* Ht.   848 *and* God restede of his worchynge] *om.* Ht.   850 ful]
om H9; fulli Ht.   854 lackiþ] wantiþ Ht.   854-855 þat þis . . . fulfillid] *om.*
Rb.   856 Crist] oure lorld Ht.   858 Orosye] Origene U.—probabyle] profitable Ht, H9, A.   861 clepid] called Rb.—sweþ] semyþ Ht; shewiþ Ra; seyþ Rb.
—last] *om.* Ht.—day] þousand Ht.   863 resoune] wordes Rb.

*Matthaeum
xxiv. (3)

*Lucam
xxi. (7)

fynde in þe gospel of Matheu þat þe disciplis axeden of 865
Crist þre questiouns: "First, what tyme þe cite of Ierusalem shulde be distroyed; þe secunde, what tokene were
of his comyge to þe dom; *and* þe þridde, what signe were
of þe ende of þe world." *And* Crist ʒaf hem no certeyn
tyme of þes þyngis whan þey schulle falle, but he ʒaf hem 870
tokenes by whyche þey myʒte wite whan þey drowen nyʒ.
And so as to þe first question of destruccion of Ierusalem
he seyde: "Whan þat þe Romaynes come to bysege þat citee,
þan sone aftir sche schulde be distroyed." And to þe secunde
and to þe þridde he ʒaf hem many tokenes þat is to seye 875
þat "rewme schulde ryse aʒens rewme, *and* peple aʒens peple,
and pestilences *and* erþe schakynges," þe whiche we haue
seye in oure dayes. But þe laste tokene þat he ʒaf was
þis: "Whan ʒe seen þe abhominacion of þe elengenesse seyd
of Danyel þe prophete stondynge on þe seyntuarie, þanne 880
whoso rede vndirstonde."

C
873 þe] *om.*
Var
out T, Hr, P, H2.
865 *in* þe gospel of Matheu] *om.* H9.   866 what tyme] when Rb.   867 tokene]
om. A.   868 to þe dom] *om.* Ht.   870 hem] *add* certeyn A.   871 drowen]
camyn Ht.   873 Whan] *add* ʒe see Rb.—þe Romaynes] *om.* A.   875 þat is to
seye] *om.* Rb.   876-878 *and* peple . . . oure dayes] et cetera Ht.   879 elen-
genesse] discoimfort Hu.
    *Matthaeum xxiv] *om.* C, Ra, Hu; *add* Matthaeum xiii Rb, H9.
    *Lucam xxi] *om.* Ht, Ra, S, C, A, Hu; Lucam 19 Rb, H9.

Vpon whiche tixte þus argueþ a doctour in a book þat
he makiþ / of þe ende of þe world: ȝif þe wordes of
Danyel han auctorite, as God seyþ þat þey haueþ, it sufficit
of noubre of ȝeeris of þe ende of þe world. Take þat Danyel   885
haþ writen. Now Daniel in þe twelþe chapitre, spekynge
of þis abhominacion, "puttiþ bytwene þe sesynge of þe bysy
sacrifice of Iewis," þe which felle whan by Titus *and*
Vaspacian Ier*usalem* was distroied, "and þe puple of Iewes
disparpullid into al þe world." *And* þis abhominacion,   890
þat doctour seiþ schal be þe grete Anticrist dayes,
"þousund two hundrid *and* nynty." Now preueþ þis doctour
þat a day mot be take here for a ȝeer, boþe by auctorite of
holy writ in þe same place and on oþre and also by resoun.
So it semeþ to þis clerk þat þe grete Anticrist schulde   895
come in þe fourtenþe hundred ȝeer fro þe birþe of Crist,
þe whiche noumbre of ȝeeris is now fulfillid not fully
twelue ȝeer and an half lackynge. Þis resoun put I not as
to schewe any certeyn tyme of his comynge, siþ y haue not

fol. 11ra

*Daniel
xij. (7-11)

C
888 by] *ins. above.*
Var
out T, Hr P, H2.
886 Now Daniel in þe twelþe chapitre] *om.* H9.—Daniel] *om.* A. 887 bysy]
holy Ht. 891 Anticrist dayes] Antecrist in þe daies of Cristis birþe H9.
897 not fully] *om.* Rb. 898 twelue ȝeer and an half lackynge] *om.* Rb.—
twelue] ten H9.—lackynge] wantynge Ht.
  *Daniel xij] *om.* C, Ra, A, T, Hr, U, Hu; *lh.* Ht.

þat knowlechynge, but to schewe þat he is nyȝ, but how   900
nyȝ I wote neuere.

fol. 11rb   But take we hede to þe / ferþ party of þe secunde
vision of Ion put in þe book of Pryuetes, in þe whiche

*Apocalyp-
sis vj   vndir openynge of seuene sealis is declarid þe staat of
holy chirche fro þe tyme of Crist into þe ende of þe world.   905
Þe openynge of þe foure first sealis scheweþ þe staat of
þe chirche fro tyme of Crist into þe tyme of Anticrist
and his forgoeris, þe whiche is schewid by þe openynge
of þe oþre þre sealis.

Þe openynge of þe first seal telleþ þe staat of þe   910
chirche in tyme of þe prechynge of Crist and of his
apostles. For þan þe first beest, þat is pe lioun, ȝaf
his vois, þat tokeneþ þe prechoures of Cristis resurrec-
(Apoc.
vi. 2)   cion and his assencion. "For þan ȝede out a whiȝt hors,
and he þat sat vpon hym had a bowe in his hond, and he   915
ȝede ouercomynge to ouercome." By þis whiȝt hors we vndir-
stondeþ þe clene lyf and conuersacion þes prechoures
hadde, and by þe bowe here trewe techynge, prickynge

Var
out T, Hr, P, H2.
901 I wote neuere] God watt Rb.   905 holy] þe Ht, S.   905-907 þe ende . . .
Crist into] *om.* Ht.   908 whiche] *add* tyme of Antecrist and his forgoeris H9.
909 þre] *om.* Ht.   910 þe staat] þe ferste stat A.   912 beest] *om.* S.   918 te-
chynge] prechinge Ht, H9.
   *Apocalypsis vj] *om.* C, Ra, Rb, S, T, Hr, A, Hu; Apocalypsis U; *lh.* Reu.
6 Ht.

sorwe i*n* me*n*nes hertis for her*e* synnes wiþoute flaterynge.
And þey wenten out of Jeuerye þ*at* þey come*n* of, ou*er*comynge 920
su*m*me of þe Jues, *and* make to leeue þe trust þ*at* þey
hadde*n* in þe olde lawe, *and* bileue i*n* I*esu* Crist, *and*
fol. 11va   sue his techynge. And þey wenten out to ou*er*co / me
þe paynemes schewynge to he*m* þat her*e* ymag*is* wer*e* none
Goddis but ma*n*nes werkes, vnmy3ty to saue he*m*self or ony 925
oþere, drawynge he*m* to þe bileue of I*esu* Crist, God *and*
ma*n*.

In þe openy*n*ge of þe secu*n*de seal, þ*er* criede þe secu*n*de beest, þ*at* is a calf, þ*at* was a beest þ*at* was woned
to be slayn *and* offrid to God i*n* þe olde lawe. þis schewiþ 930
þe staat of þe chirche in tyme of martiris, þ*at* for stede-
fast p*re*chy*n*g of trewþe *and* trewe Goddis lawe schedde her*e*
blod. þ*at* is signified by þe rede hors þ*at* wente out at
þis seal openy*n*ge. And þis staat byga*n* in þe tyme of Nero,
þe c*u*rsed emp*er*our, *and* durede i*n* þe tyme of Co*n*stantyne 935
þe Gr*e*te þ*at* enduede þe chirche. For in his tyme many of
Cristis seruaunt*is* *and* namely þe lederes of Goddis folk
wer*e* slayn. For of two and twenty bischopes of Rome þ*at*

C
920 of] *om.*   929 þat was woned] *om.* þat.   936 in] *om.*—many] namely.
Var
out T, Hr, P, H2.
919 wiþoute flaterynge] *om.* Rb.   920 out of . . . come*n* of] *om.* Rb.   923 sue]
see Ht; shewe Ra; *om.* H9.   925 saue] helpyn Ht.   931-932 stedefast] trewe
Rb.   932 of trewþe *and* trewe] *om.* Rb, Hu.   933 signified] bytoknyd Ht.—
rede] þredde A; 3ridde U.   934 in þe tyme of] *om.* Ht.   937 namely þe] *om.* Ht.

weren bytwen Petir *and* Siluestre þe firste, I rede but of
foure þat ne wer*en* martiris for þe lawe of Crist. And   940
also i*n* þe tyme of Dioclician þe emp*erour*, þe p*er*secucio*un*
vpon C*risten* men was so gret þat wiþi*nn*e þretty dayes þ*er*
were two *and* twenty þousand me*n and* wy*mm*en slayn by diu*er*se
fol. 11ᵛᵇ cou*n*trees / for Goddis sake.

    Þe openyge of þe þridde seal telleþ þe staat of þe   945
chirche i*n* tyme of her*e*tikes, þat beþ fygured by þe blake
hors for fals vndirsto*n*dynge of holy writ. For þa*n* criede
þe þridde best þat is a ma*n*. For at þat tyme was it nede
to p*r*eche þe misterie of C*ristis* incarnacion *and* his pas-
sioun toꝛens þese her*e*tikis, þat felede mys of þes poyntes: 950
how Crist toke v*er*ey ma*n*nes kynde of our*e* lady, hym beynge
God as he was byfore, *and* his modr*e* beynge maide byfore
and aftir.

    Þe openy*n*ge of þe ferþe seal telliþ þe staat of þe
chirche i*n* tyme of ypocritis, þat þen signified by þe pale   955
hors, þat beþ sygnes of penau*n*se wiþoute forþ to bly*n*de
þe puple. "And he þat sat vpon þis hors, his name was deeþ."

Var
out T, Hr, P, H2.
939 þe firste] *om.* Rb, A. 940 of Crist] of Iesu Crist A. 946 blake] pale Ht.
949-950 passiou*n*] *add* to men H9. 951-953 how . . . aftir] *om.* Ht. 955 sig-
nified] bitoknyd Ht. 956 beþ] maken Rb.

For þey schulle sle gostly he*m* þat þey lede*n and* techiþ
(Apoc. vi. 8) to trist vpon oþre þyng þan God. "*And* helle folewiþ hym,"　　　960
for helle r*e*sceyueþ þilke þat þese disceyueþ. At þat time
schal it nede þat þe firþe best, þat is þe egle, make his
cry, þat fleþ hyʒest of foules to rer*e* vp Goddis gospel
and to pr*e*yse þat lawe aboue oþere, laste ma*n*nes wit *and*
fol. 12ʳᵃ here tradic*i*ons ou*e*rgoo *and* trede dou*n* / þe lawe of God　　　965
by enformynge of þes ypocrites. *And* þis is þe laste staat
þat is or schal be in þe chirche byfore þe comynge of gr*e*te
An*t*icrist.

þe openynge of þe fifte seal telliþ þe stat of þe
chirche þat þan schal folewe and þe desir þat loueris of
Goddis lawe schulleþ haue aft*ir* þe ende of þis world to be　　　970
delyuer*e*d of þis woo.

þe openy*n*g of þe sixte seal telleþ þe staat of þe
chirche i*n* tyme of An*t*icris*t*is lymes, þe whiche staat ʒe
mowe knowe to be in þe chirche wha*n* ʒe seeþ fulfillid þat
*Apocalip-sis vij. (1) Seynt Jon propheci*e*þ to falle on þe openy*n*ge of þis, wher*e*　　　975
he seiþ þus: "Aft*ir* þis y seye four*e* au*n*gelis sto*n*dynge
vpon four*e* corner*i*s of þe erþe, holdynge þe foure wyndes

Var
out T, Hr, P, H2.
958-959 þey lede*n* . . . to] *om.* Rb.　959 trist] Crist Ra.　960 for helle . . .
disceyueþ] *om.* Ht, Rb.　961 firþe] *om.* Rb.—egle] eren H9.　962 Goddis]
Cristes U.　963 oþere] *add* lawes Hu.　964 *and* trede dou*n*] *om.* Ht.　970
Goddis lawe] *add* and þe ioʒe þat þei Rb.　970-971 to be delyuered of þis woo]
om. H9.　972 seal] *om.* U.　974 fulfillid] *om.* Ht.　975 Jon] *add* þe evangelist
H9.—þis] þe sixte seal H9; þis seel Ht, Hu.　977 corner*i*s] *om.* H9; *lh. insert*
wyndes H9.—holdynge þe foure wyndes] *om.* Hu.
　　*Apocalipsis vij] *om.* C, Ra, Rb, S, T, Hr, A, Hu.

of þe erþe þat þey blowe nouȝt vpon þe erþe ne vpon þe
see ne vpon any tree." Þese foure aungelis beþ þe noubre
of alle þe dewellis mynistris þat in þat tyme schulleþ in   980
plesaunce of here lord Anticrist stoppe þe foure wyndes,
þat beþ þe foure gospellis to be prechid, *and* so lette þe
breþ of þe grace of þe holy gost to falle vpon men mornynge
for synne *and* castynge hem to amendement, *and* ouþer vpon
hem þat wolde encresse in vertues, ouþer vpon parfyte men.   985

fol. 12ʳᵇ   What is þer aftir þys to falle but / þat þe mysterie
of þe seuenþe seal be schewid, þat he come into his owne
*II Thes-   persone, "þat Iesu Crist shal slee wiþ spirit of his mouþ"
salonicen-
ses ii   whan þe fend schal schewe þe vttermest persecucion þat
capitulo.   he *and* his seruauntis may do to Cristes lymes; *and* þat   990
(8)
schal be þe þridde warnyng þat þe world schal haue to come
to þis dredful dom. In al þis mater haue y nouȝt seid of
myself, but of oþere doctoures þat beþ preued.

      I seyde also in my secunde principal, þat it were to
wite tofore what iuge we schulde rekene, werfore we schulle   995

Var
out T, Hr, P.   978-986 of þe erþe . . . to falle H2.
978 of þe erþe] *om.* Ht, Hu.   979 any] *om.* Ht; þe U.   982-983 þe breþ of] *om.*
Ht.   985 ouþer vpon parfyte men] *om.* Rb.   987 he] þe grete Antecrist H9.
988 mouþ] *add* as Poul seiþ Rb.   990 he *and*] *om.* A, H2.—lymes] seruauntes
Rb, Hu.   992 dom] *add* where þou shalt ȝelde rekenynge of þi bailie H9.
994 secunde] *om.* Hu.
      *II Thessalonicenses ii capitulo] *om.* C, Ht, Ra, Rb, S, T, H9, Hr, A,
Hu, H2.

wite þat God hymself schal heren þis rekenynge, he þat seeþ
alle oure dedes *and* alle oure þouȝtis fro þe bygynnynge
of oure lyf to þe ende. And he schal schewe þere þe hidde
þyngis of oure herte, openynge to al þe world þe riȝtfulnesse of his dom. So þat wiþ þe myȝt of God euery mannys   1000
dedis to al þe world schal be schewid.

    And so it semeþ by þe wordis of Seynt Jon in þe book

*Apocalip-
sis xx.
(12)
of Priueytes, þer he seiþ þus: "I seye dede men, littul *and*
grete, stondynge in þe syȝt of þe trone. *And* bookes weren
opened. And anoþer book was opened þat was of lyf. *And*   1005
dede men weren iuged aftir þe þyngis þat weren writen in

fol. 12va
þe bookis aftir here wer / chynges." Þese bokes beþ mennis
conciensis, þat now beþ closed; but þan þey schulleþ ben
opened to al þe world to rede þerinne, boþe dedis *and*
þoutis. But þe book of lif is Cristis lyuynge *and* doctrine   1010
þat is now hid to men þat shulleþ be dampned þouȝ here owne
malice, þat demeþ men to swe þe world raþere þan God. In

C
1005 And anoþer book was opened] *om.*
Var
out T, Hr, P.
1000 dom] wisdom H9.   1005 And anoþer book was opened] *om.* Ra.
1007 aftir] of A, H2.   1009 þerinne] *om.* Ht.   1010 Cristis] *add* techynge and
Hu.   1011-1012 þouȝ here . . . þan God] *om.* Rb.
   *Apocalipsis xx] *om.* C, Ra, S, A, T, Hr, Hu, H2; Apocalipsis Rb; Reu.
1 Ht.

þe first bok schal be write al þat we haue do; in þe toþer
book schal be write þat we schulde haue do. *And* þan shulle
dede me*n* be demed of þilke þyng*is* þat beþ write*n* in þe   1015
bookis. For ʒif þo dedis þat we haueþ do, þe whiche beþ
write*n* in þe bokis of our*e* co*n*science, be acordynge to þe
book of Cr*is*tis techynge *and* his lyuy*n*ge, þe whiche is þe
bok of lyf, we schulleþ be saued; *and* ellis we schulleþ
be da*m*pned. For þe dom schal be ʒoue aft*ir* oure werkis.   1020

    Loke þ*er*fore now what þyng is write*n* in þe bok of þy
co*n*science whyle þou art here. *And* ʒif þou fyndest out
co*n*trarie to Cr*is*tis lif oþer to his techynge, wiþ þe knyf
of penau*n*ce *and* r*e*pentau*n*ce scrape it awey, *and* write it
beterer, eu*er*more hertily þynkynge þat þou schalt ʒelde   1025
rekeny*n*ge of þy baylie.

    Also y seyde principaly þat it wer*e* to wite what re-
fol. 12vb ward schal be ʒouen in þat / dom to wyse seruantis *and*
goode, and what to false seruauntis *and* wickede. For þe
whiche it is to wite þat our*e* lord I*esu* Crist schal come to   1030
þe dom here i*n* þis world i*n* þe same body þat he tok of our*e*

C
1021 þy] *om.* 1029 to] *om.*
Var
out 1013-1026 T, Hr, P.
1013 bok] *lh. mg.* Hu. 1013-1014 schal be write . . . toþer book] *om.* Ht.
1016 bookis] *add* of oure conscience Rb. 1017 þe bokis of oure] *om.* H2, A.
1023-1024 wiþ þe knyf . . . scrape it awey] *om.* A. 1024 *and* repentau*n*ce] *om.*
Ht. 1025 hertily] *om.* Ht, Hu.—ʒelde] ʒeue A, H2. 1027 principaly] *om.* Ht.
1028 in þat dom] *om.* Hu.—dom] day Ht. 1030-1031 to þe dom here] *om.* T,
Hr, P.

lady, hauynge þerinne þe woundes þat he suffrede for oure
aȝen-byggynge. *And* al þat euere schul be saued, takynge

*(I) Thes-
salonicen-
ses iiij.
(17)

aȝen here bodies, clyuynge to here heed Crist, schulle be
rauyssched, "metyng hym in þe aiere," as Poul seyþ.   1035
Þey þat schulle be dampned lyuynge vpon þe erþe as
in a tounne of wyn dregges dwelliþ byneþe, and þe clere
wyn hoouereþ aboue. Þanne schal Crist axke rekeninge of
þe dedis of mercy, reprouynge fals Cristene men for þe
leuynge of hem, rehersynge þe dedis of þe same *and* oþre   1040
trewþis, by þe whiche his trewe seruauntis haue folewede
hym. Þanne schulle þilke false seruauntis goo wiþ þe deuel,
whom þey haue serued, þe erþe hem swelwynge into þe endeles fier. And ryȝtful men schullen go into euerelastynge
lyf.   1045

*Apocalyp-
sis viij. (13)
fol. 13ʳᵃ

Þan schal be fulfillid þat is writen in þe bok of
Pryueytes: "Woo, woo, / wo to hem þat dwelleþ in þe erþe."
Wo to þe paynyme, þat ȝaf þat worchipe to dede ymagis wrouȝt

C
1034 heed] *om.*
Var
out 1042-1048 wiþ þe deuel . . . wrouȝt Hu.
1032 lady] *add* Seynte Marie A, H2; *add* Marie P. 1032-1033 hauynge . . .
aȝen] *repeat* Hr. 1034 heed] *add* Iesu A, H2. 1038 hoouereþ] *om.* H9.
1039 reprouyng] *add* alle P. 1040 of þe same] *om.* Rb; of merci Ht.—oþre]
here A, H2. 1041 trewþis] *add* fulfilled P.—folewede] filled T, Hr. 1048 ȝaf]
haue Ht.
    *Thessalonicenses iiij] *in text* P; *om.* C, Ht, Ra, Rb, S, T, H9, Hr, A, Hu;
Thessalonicenses H2.
    *Apocalypsis viij] *in text* P; *om.* C, Ht, Ra, Rb, A, S, Hu, H2.

of mennes hondis, *and* to oþer creatures þat he schulde
haue ȝoue to God þat hym wrouȝte. Wo to þe Iewe, þat   1050
tristed so moche in þe olde lawe; þan schal he see Marie
sone demynge þe world, whom he despised *and* sette on þe
cros. Wo to þe false Cristene man, þat knewe þe wille of
his Lord *and* fulfillid it not.

Also wo for synne of þynkyng to þe þat hast schit out   1055
þe mayne of God, þat is mynde of his passioun, holy con-
templacion of his godnesse *and* memorie of his benfetis,
fro þe chaumbre of þyn herte, *and* hast maad it an hous of
swyn *and* a den of þeues by vnclene þouȝtes *and* delitis.
As þou here hast spered God out of þyn hert, so he schal   1060
spere þe out of heuene. Þou hast herberwed þe meyne of
þe fend, *and* wyþ hem in helle þou schalt euere abyde.

Wo also for synne of speche, for þou myȝt not opene
þilke foule *and* stynkynge mouþ, wiþ þe whiche þou schalt
speke vnhoneste cursynge, fraude, disceyt, lesynges, for-   1065
fol. 13ʳᵇ   sweryng, scornynge, / and bacbitynge, to plese God in þe
felaschipe of seyntis. For louynge is not commeliche in

Var
out Hu.
1050 ȝoue] don Rb.   1053 false] *om.* T, Hr.   1054 Lord] God Ht.   1056
mayne] name T, Hr, P.—is] *add* to sey T, Hr, P.   1056-1057 holy contempla-
cion] þe byholdyng T, Hr, P.   1057 benfetis] charite T, Hr, P.   1058 fro þe
chaumbre of þyn herte] *om.* T, Hr, P.   1059 swyn] synne P.—*and* delitis] *om.*
Ht.   1060 spered] schyt Ht, T, H9, Hr, P; spared Rb.   1061 spere] schyt Ht,
T, H9, Hr, P; spare Rb.   1062 in helle] *om.* Rb.   1064 foule *and*] *om.* Hr; false
H9.—foule *and* stynkynge] *om.* P.   1063-1065 for þou . . . vnhoneste] for with
þat mowth þat þou hast vsed here in erthe to lesyngges and to Rb.   1065 vn-
honeste] *add* speeches U.—cursynge] *add* to swerynges in Rb.—disceyt] dispite
T, Hr, U, P.   1065-1066 disceyt, . . . forsweryng] begylyngges Rb.   1066 bac-
bitynge] *add* and oþur vnclene spekynges þou may neuer Rb.   1066-1067 in
þe felaschipe of] amonge þe blissed Rb.   1067 seyntis] *add* in heven Rb.—
louynge] praysyng T, Hr, A, P, H2; *add* or preisynge H9; *add* of God Rb.—
commeliche] semly T, H9, Hr, P.

mowþis of synneris. For in þe whiche, ȝif þou haddist
kep þy mouþe clene, þou schuldest haue songe in heuene

*Apocalip-
sis iiij.
(8)*
in felachipe of angelis þys blissed song: "Sanctus, sanctus,   1070
sanctus, dominus deus omnipotens"; holy, holy, holy, Lord
God Almyȝty. Þan ȝellynge *and* wepynge, þou schalt crye in
cumpanye of deueles: ve, ve, ve, quante sunt tenebre;
wo, wo, wo, how grete beþ þes derkenessis.

Wo also for synne of dede. Þou hast be proud. "Þy   1075

*Isaias
(xiv. 15)
*Sapientia
ij. (24-25)*
pride schal be drawe to helle," as Ysaye seyþ. Or þou hast
be brent wiþ envye. "Þouȝ enuye of þe deuel, enuye entrid
into þe world, *and* þey schulleþ folewe hym þat beþ on his
syde," as Salamon seyþ. Or þou hast be styred wiþ wraþe.

*Matthaeum
v. (22)*
"*And* eueryche man þat beryþ wraþþe to his broþer is gilty   1080
in dom," as Crist seyþ in þe gospel of Matheu. Or þou hast

C
1069 þou] *om.*   1075 dede] *add* þat.—be] *mg.*
Var
out Hu.
1068 in þe whiche] *om.* Rb, U.   1069 clene] *add* with opur dew obseruances
Rb.   1070 felachipe] companye Rb.—of] *add* seyntis T, H9, Hr, P.   1071 deus
omnipotens] saboath Rb.   1072 Almyȝty] *add* for but for defawte of clene
kepynge of þi mowth and vsynge of þe vices aforesaid Rb.   1073 deueles]
fendes Rb.—tenebre] *add* þat is Ht, A, H2, Hu; *add* þat is to seie P.   1074
grete] muche T, Hr, P.   1077 deuel] *add* and with T, Hr, P.—enuye] deþ Rb,
H2; *add* of hym deþ P.   1077-1079 þouȝ enuye . . . as Salamon seyþ. Or] *om.*
Ht.   1078-1079 and þey . . . syde] *om.* H2.   1079 seyþ] *add* imitantur eum qui
sunt ex parte eius P.   1081 of Matheu] *om.* Rb.
     *Apocalipsis iiij] *om.* C, Ht, Ra, S, T, H9, Hr, A, Hu, P, H2; Apocalipsis
Rb.
     *Isaias] *om.* C, Ht, Ra, S, T, H9, Hr, A, Hu, P, H2.
     *Sapientia ij] *om.* C, Ht, Ra, S, T, Hr, A, U, Hu, P, H2.
     *Matthaeum v] *om.* C, Ra, S, T, H2, Hr, A, Hu, P; *lh.* Ht.

Proverbia iij. (vi. 11)   be slow to goode dedis. "Myssayse schal come to þe as a weyferynge man, *and* þy pouert as a man armed," as þe book of P*r*ouerbis seiþ. Or þou hast haunted lecherye, glotonye

*fol. 13*ᵛᵃ   oþer coueytyse. þat for / soþe wite ʒe þat "eueriche   1085

Ephesios v. (5)   auoutir oþer vnclene man þat is gloton oþer chynche schal neu*er*e haue heritage in þe r*e*wme of Crist *and* of God," as Poul seyþ. "But fier, brymston, *and* þe spirit of tempestis,

Psalmo x. (7)   þat is þe fend of helle, schulleþ be a party of here peyne," as it is write in þe Sauter*e*.   1090

Whan þese dampned men beþ in þis woo þey schulleþ

(Lamenta-tiones v. 15-16)   synge þis rewful song þat is writen in þe Book of Mornynge:

þe ioye of oure herte is ago;

Oure wele is turned into woo;

þe coroune of oure heued is falle vs fro;   1095

Alas for synne þat we haue doo.

C
1096 haue] *om.*
Var
out Hu.
1082 dedis] workys U.—Myssayse] desesys T, Hr, P. 1082-1084 as a wey-ferynge . . . seiþ] *om.* Rb. 1083 *and* þy pouert as a man] *om.* A, H2. 1084 haunted lecherye] ben stered wiþ lecherie oþer haunted P. 1085 ʒe] *add* well A, H2. 1086 þat is gloton oþer chynche] *om.* Rb. 1087 *and* of God] *om.* Rb˙ 1088 fier] *add* of Helle Hr, P.—spirit]; gost T, Hr, P. 1090 as it is . . . Sauter*e*] *om.* Ht; *add* þus ignis sulphur, and spiritus procellarum pars calicis eorum P. 1094 wele] myrþe Ht; song T, H9, Hr, P, H2; velle Rb; quere A, Ra, S; quiet U.
     Proverbia iij] om. Ht, Ra, S, T, H9, Hr, C, A, U, Hu, P, H2.
     Ephesios v] om. C, Ht, Ra, S, T, Hr, A, Hu.
     Psalmo x] om. C, Ht, Ra, S, A, H9, Hu; Psalmo viij T, Hr.

But ioye *and* ioye *and* ioye to hem þat beþ saued—ioye in
God, ioye in hemself, ioye in oþre þat beþ saued. Also
ioye for her trauayle is brouȝt to so graciouns an ende,
ioye for þey beþ scaped þe peyne of helle, ioye for þe
endeless blisse þat þey haue in syȝt of God.

1100

Cui sit honor *et* gloria in secula seculorum. Amen.

C
1097 beþ] deþ. 1100 þe peyne] *om*. þe.
Var
out Hu.
1097 *and* ioye to] *om*. and ioye T, A, H2, Hr. 1099 graciouns] semyng Ht.
1102 Cui . . . Amen] To whom be worshipe and glorie into worldis of
worldis. Amen H2; To whom be honoure and glorie into þe worldlis of
worldlis, and he vs graunt þerof þis joye parte. Amen T, Hr, P; to whom be
honour and glorie into þe world of worldis and graunte vs þerwiþ to parte.
Amen. It endiþ H9.

Chapter VIII

NOTES

Passages quoted or paraphrased from the Vulgate Bible are identified in the Marginalia of the Sermon. Additional data to that found in the Manuscript are put in parentheses.

1 The subject of the sermon—Give account of your stewardship—is repeated in Additional MS. 21253, f. 130 ff. See G. W. Owst, *Preaching in Medieval England* (Cambridge, 1926), p. 339.

13-26 Although I have been unable to locate the source of this interpretation, I have found similar allegorical explication in the Biblical exegesis of the time. Hugh of St. Victor ["Allegoriae in Novum Testamentum," Bk. II, ch. xxx. J. P. Migne, *Patrologiae Cursus Completus, Series Latina* (Paris, 1882), CLXXV, col. 797] suggests several explanations, one being: "Homo paterfamilias, est Deus; vinea, Ecclesia; operarii, praelati; horae diei, aetas saeculi." Nicholas de Lyra [*Moralia Super Totam Biblium* (Mantua, 1481), Mathaeus xx] explains the hours of the day as the ages of man: childhood, youth, manhood, old age, while the *Glossa Ordinaria* [Migne, *PL*, CXIV, col. 150] suggests that the vine is the universal church whose laborers range from Abel to the last of the elect.

27-56 Owst [*Literature and Pulpit in Medieval England* (Cambridge, 1933), pp. 549-551] compares the interpretation of the parable here with ideas of St. Anselm and even of Plato in Book II of *The Republic*. He refers the reader to several other sermons: Lincoln Cathedral MS. A.6.2, ff. 67b-68b; Additional MS. 41321, f. 65.

38-56 This conception of the three estates and of the need of each for the other was not peculiar to Thomas Wymbledon. John Bromyard, for example, in his "Compassionis," [*Summa Praedicantium* (Basel, 1484)], enjoins each estate to help and support the other. "Operarium laboribus; miles defensionibus; clericus orationibus; et in istis artibus sic alternari debent; quod ubi unus deficit, alius suppleat."

Owst, in *Preaching in Medieval England* (p. 264), refers to processional and open-air sermons in which sections are addressed to the three estates. Bromyard, Rypon, Brunton, and Myrc are among the writers mentioned. In *Literature and Pulpit* (pp. 552-564), Owst shows how medieval sermons emphasize the idea of the necessity of class distinctions and class duties.

57 Avicenna, *De Anima: A Compendium on the Soul*, tr. Edward Abbott van Dyck (Verona, Italy, 1906), sect. ix, p. 86.

123-126 The interest manifested here in the Judgment Day is typical of many medieval preachers. Owst (*Lit. and Pulpit*, pp. 521-524) refers the reader to many other works; among these are the *Towneley Plays*, *Pricke of Conscience*, and Bromyard's *Summa Praedicantium*.

145-147 John Bromyard, in "Ordo Clericalis," *SP*, specifies four questions: "quomodo intrastis, quomodo vixistis, quomodo resistis, quomodo bona ecclesie expenditis."

In a sermon on the same text, Bodleian MS. 406, f. 439, priests are asked three questions: "Quis te huc adduxit? Quid hic agis? Quam ob causam huc venire voluisti?"

A similar passage is found in *Speculum Christiani*, ed. Gustaf Holmstedt [(London, 1933), EETS, CLXXXII, 54, 55]: "Euery man shal ȝelde up a streyte a-cownte and reson be-for god of al thynges that he has doon or spoken; be whych helpes, bi what meryte, and by what entente he has comen to any state or degre; hou he has entrede, hou he has lyuede, hou he has perseuerede; what he has lernede, what he has taught, and in what doctrine he has continuede . . . quomodo intrauit, quomodo vixit, quomodo perseueravit."

151-156 Compare Gregorius, "Moralium" Liber xvi, ch. 73, paragraph 83 (Migne, *PL*, LXXVI, col. 1160), a sentence of which is quoted in a Latin Manuscript of this sermon, *Ul*, f. 141ʳ, "Peccatum quippe usque ad inferos ducitur, quod ante finem vitae praesentis per correctionem ad poenitentiam non emendatur."

164-166 With this section on worldly interests of the priests, compare William Langland, *Piers Plowman*, B Text, "Prologue," 83-111.

187-190 Owst (*Preaching in Medieval England*, pp. 32-33) notes many references in medieval literature to the decay and neglect of theology in schools.

196-205 I have been unable to locate this quotation in Chrysostome's sermons. This admonition to parents concerning the training of children is frequently found in medieval homiletical literature, as *Handlynge Synne*, Bromyard's *Summa Praedicantium*, and sermons by Rypon and Brunton. See Owst, *Lit. and Pulpit*, pp. 461-468.

See also William Langland, *Piers Plowman*, B text, Passus v, 34-41.

206 ff. Not only Wycliffites but also the orthodox ecclesiastics were advocating reform within the church; there were Mannyng, Bromyard, Rypon, Myrc, William of Rymyngton, William de Pagula, Gasquet, and others. See Owst, *Lit. and Pulpit*, pp. 268-281; *Preaching in Med. England*, pp. 32-47, 125.

212 Book of Mornynge is *Lamentations* of Jeremiah.

235-238 Same question is asked of prelates in Bromyard, "Ordo Clericalis," *S.P.*

248-259 Bernardus of Clairvaux, "Sermones in Cantica," Migne, *PL*, CLXXXIII, col. 891.

277-280 Although I have been unable to locate this passage, it may possibly have reference to the following sentences in Hugh of St. Victor's "Allegoriae in Vetus Testamentum," Bk. III, ch. i (Migne, *PL*, CLXXV, col. 654, 655):

> Lutum in quo servierunt filii Israel Pharaoni, eo quod lutum inquivat, luxuriam designat. Palea, eo quod levis est, et cito transvolat, vanam gloriam significat. Later quoque, qui de molli terra confectus, per decoctionem ignis durescit, humani cordis duritiam, per longam sive concupiscentiae, sive libidinis aut avaritiae consuetudinem decoctam ostendit.

Owst (*Preaching in Med. England*, p. 163) suggests that Hugh of St. Victor was quoting St. Jerome; he compares this interpretation to similar passages in other medieval works, among them *Jacob's Well*, *Piers Plowman*, and sermons in Lincoln Cathedral MS. A. 6. 2.

315-317 Aristotle, "Ethica Nicomachea," Liber VIII, cap. x, *Opera Omnia Graece et Latine* (Paris, 1850), II, 99.

356-368 Compare S. Isidore Hispalensis Episcopi, *Sententiarum*, Liber III, "De Judicibus," cap. lii, no. 11 (Migne, LXXXIII, col 725):

> Saepe judices pravi cupiditatis causa aut differunt, aut pervertunt judicia; nec finiunt coepta parcium negotia, quousque marsupia eorum qui causantur, exhauriant. Quando enim judicant, non causam, sed dona considerant; et sicut negligentes sunt in discussione causantium, sic eorum damno solliciti sunt."

The first sentence of the above is quoted in the University Library MS. Ii III 8 after line 197.

380-382 Gregorius I, "Moralium," Liber xxiv, cap. 25, paragraph 54, Migne, *PL*, LXXVI, col. 318.

410-415 S. Aurelius Augustinus, "Sermone lxxv," Migne, *PL*, XXXIX, Appendix, col. 1890.

416-418 Gregorius I, "Moralium," Liber xv, cap. 25, Migne, *PL*, LXXV, col. 1095.

419-554 These lines are quoted in part by Owst, (*Lit. and Pulpit*, pp. 93-94), who gives parallel passages in other sermons among which are sermons in Salisbury Cathedral Library MS. 103 and in Gloucester Cathedral Library MS. (15th century Homilies) Sermon for 5th Sunday after Trinity.

435 ff. This interpretation is quite similar to that found in Gregorius, "Moralium," Liber xiv, cap. 53, Migne, *PL*, LXXV, col. 1072-1074. See also Nicholas de Lyra, *Moralia, op. cit.*, Zacharias v.

444-445 Bartholomeus, *De Proprietalibus Rerum*, tr. John Trevisa (London, 1535), Bk. xii, ch. 27. The Latin text of the Cambridge University Library manuscript gives a clue to this reference in saying, "ut ait Bartholomus, libro 15, capitulo 97."

Both Bromyard and Rypon refer to nightbirds as lovers of darkness and of dark deeds. See Owst, *Lit. and Pulpit*, p. 240.

460-468 Owst, in *Literature and Pulpit*, pp. 93-95, identifies these two women as the devil's daughters, about whom there was considerable allegoric narration in thirteenth century French sermons. See also Barthélemy Hauréau's article in *Journal des Savants*, Vol. for 1884, pp. 225-228. *Jacob's Well* has a similar interpretation of the verse from Proverbs; see *Jacob's Well*, ed. Arthur Brandeis (London, 1900), Pt. I, ch. xxi, pp. 145-146.

468-470 Gregorius, *Regulae Pastoralis Liber*, cap. xix, Migne, *PL*, LXXVII, col. 81.

470-474 Augustinus, *Liber de Conflictu Vitiorum et Virtutum*, cap. xiv, Migne, *PL*, XL, col. 1098. Compare Chaucer, "Pardoner's Tale," lines 485-487, *Canterbury Tales*.

475-476 Bartholomeus, *De Proprietalibus Rerum*, Liber xii, cap. 26.

477-489 Augustinus, "Sermone," no. 367, Migne, *PL*, XXXIX, col. 1651. There is a similar interpretation in Innocent III's *De Contemptu Mundi*, Liber II, cap. vi-vii, Migne, *PL*, CCXVII, col. 719-720.

485-510 Similar ideas concerning avarice are to be found in Bromyard, "Avaricia," *S.P.;* he also quotes Innocent and Augustine.

Owst considers the terminology in lines 504-505 to connect this passage with the Peasants' Revolt of 1382. See Owst, *Lit. and Pulpit*, pp. 305-306; 318-319.

492-503 Innocentius, *De Contemptu Mundi sive De Miseria Conditionis Humanae*, Liber II, cap. ix., Migne, *PL*, CCXVII, col. 720.

504-541 Quoted in Owst, *Literature and Pulpit*, pp. 350-306.

515-537 Ambrosius, *De Nabuthae*, Migne, *PL*, XIV, col. 770.

542-546 Gregorius, "Moralium," Liber xiv, cap. 53, Migne, *PL*, LXXV, col. 1073.

584-601 This grim picturing of death was a common medieval device. See Owst, *Lit. and Pulpit*, pp. 531, 532; *Meditations of St. Bernard*, Migne, *PL*, CLXXXIV, col. 485.

593-601 Bromyard, "Vocatio," *S.P.*, lists the three messengers as persecution, nakedness, and hunger, who "allicit," "trahit," and "impellit."

Owst, in *Lit. and Pulpit*, p. 532, relates the dramatic personification in this passage to that in several other medieval works. See *Everyman; Messagers of Deeth*, (EETS, OS, no. 117, pp. 443-448); *Pricke of Conscience*, 11. 1865-1889.

657 The Gloss referred to in several places I have been unable to identify. It is not *Glossa Ordinaria*, ascribed to Walafrid Strabo, or Peter Lombard's *Magna Glosatura*, or *Media Glosature* by Anselm of Laon.

698 "þat he was heuy þerwiþ and myȝt nouȝt suffre it"

There are so many *variae lectiones* for this reading that it is difficult to decide what the original reading may have been. Therefore, I have chosen for the basic text the reading of *C*. See above, Section V: "The text and Editorial Principles."

The source, II Machabaeorum ix. 10, reads: "Et qui paulo ante sidera caeli contingere se arbitrabatur, eum nemo poterat propter intolerantiam fetoris portare." Thus, for the correct meaning, the text should read: þat he was heuy þerwiþ and his frendis myȝt not suffre it.

725-727 This description of an old man appears again and again in literature; one immediately thinks of Chaucer's Reeve as he is described in the Prologue to the Reeve's Tale. Perhaps many of these depictions of age were influenced by that found in De *Duodecim Abusionum Gradibus*, attributed to many writers, among whom was Augustine:

> Dum oculi caligant, aures graviter audiunt, capilli fluunt, facies in pallorem mutatur, dentes lapsi numero minuintur, cutis arescit, flatus non suaviter oler, pectus suffocatur, tussis cachivat, genua trepidant, talos et pedes tumor inflat, etiam homo interior qui non senescit, his omnibus aggravatur. Et haec omnia ruituram jamjamque domum corporis cito praenuntiant. Quid ergo superest, nisi ut dum hujus vitae defectus appropriat, nihil aliud cogitare, quam quomodo futurae vitae aditus propere comprehendatur, quisque senex appetat?
>
> Migne. *PL*, XL, col. 1079-1080

Owst, in *Preaching in Medieval England*, p. 342, tells of a similar passage in many writers, among whom are Bromyard, in "Mors," *S.P.*, and Myrc, in *Festiall*.

737-738 This reference I could not locate. In *De Duodecim Abusionum Gradibus*, attributed to Augustine, we read:

> Secundus abusionis gradus est, si sine religione senex esse inveniatur: cui cum membra exterioris hominis veterascunt, vires animi, id est, interioris hominis membra, incremata roboris non capiunt.
>
> Migne, *PL*, XL, col. 1079.

757-760 Augustinus, Epistola 199 (alias 80), Migne, *PL*, XXXIII, col. 905.

824-836 Joannis Chrysostomus, *Opus Imperfectum*, Hom. xxxiv, Migne, *PL*, LVI, col. 818. Bromyard, *Summa Praedicantium*, "Judicii divini," also quotes this passage.

830 "first in þe" (*A, Hu*), although the minority reading, is selected for the reconstructed text for clarity of thought; "in," the word in question, is also found in the source of the passage.

837-840 The exposition of Jeremiah I have been unable to locate. Miss Smalley states that there was a spurious commentary of Jeremiah ascribed to Joachim. See Beryl Smalley, *The Study of the Bible in the Middle Ages* (Oxford, 1941), 228.

841-851 S. Hildegarde, *Scivias sive Visionum ac Revelationum*, Book III, Vision xi, Migne, *PL*, CXCVIII, col. 714-715.

859-861 I have been unable to locate this reference in *Speculum Judiciale*.

873-874 Lucam xxi. 20.

876-877 Lucam xxi. 10-11; Matthaeum xxiv. 7.

879-881 Matthaeum xxiv. 15.

882-894 This "doctour" I have been unable to identify.

910-993 This interpretation of the opening of the seven seals is exactly the same as that given by Richard of St. Victor, *In Apocalypsim Libri System*, Liber II, cap. iv-x, Migne, *PL*, CXCVI, col. 759-775. It is likely that this book is the source of the author's interpretation. However, although I have been unable to locate a similar explication, the interpretation may have been one rather generally accepted at the time. Quite different are the explanations given by Nicholas of Lyra and Abbot Joachim. Nicholas of Lyra in his *Moralia* interprets the horses as the seven deadly sins. Abbot Joachim, in *Super Apocalipsim* (Venetia, 1527), explains that the four animals represent the four orders of perfection: apostles, martyrs, confessors or doctors, and virgins or hermits; the seven seals represent the seven eras of persecution: in Judea, in Rome, in Greece, in Parthia, in "Theogonia," "in Soldano," in Italy. Parts of Joachim's explication are similar to the sermon's interpretation, but the total explanation is very different.

929 For the identification of the beasts of the first four seals see Apocalipsis iv. 7.

933-934 Apocalipsis vi. 4.

945-947 Apocalipsis vi. 5.

956; 959 Apocalipsis vi. 8.

1093-1096 Lamentationes Ieremi*ae* v. 15-16:

> Defecit gaudium cordis nostri
>   versus est in luctum chorus noster,
> cecidit corona capitis nostri;
>   vae nobis, quia peccavimus!

Parallels to this lyric are cited in Carlton Brown, *A Register of Middle English Religious and Didactic Verse*. (Oxford, 1916), II, 326. Two of these from the Harley MS. 7322 are quoted below:

Harley 7322, f. 153 v. *Political, Religious, and Love Poems*, ed. Frederick J. Furnivall (EETS-OS, 15), p. 261:

> Al þe ioȝe of oure herte nou is went a-wey
> for into serwe and into wo, tornid is al oure pley.
> þe croune of oure heved is felle to gronde:
> þat euere we sennede, welawey þe stonde.

Harley 7322, f. 172 v. *Pol., Rel. and Love Poems*, p. 268:

> Strong it þus to flitte
> Fro worldes blisse to pitte;
> Strengore is to misse
> Heuene-riche blisse
> Strengest is to wende
> To pine wit-outen ende.
> þe blisse of oure herte, al it is ago;
> Al ure wele torned is to wo
> þe croune of ure heved
> Fallen is to grounde:
> þat we euer syngeden
> Wellawey þe stounde!

1094 wele: There are so many variant readings for this word that I have chosen the *C* reading for the text, although "quere" occurs in more manuscripts than any other of the *variae lectiones*.

IX. GLOSSARY

The glossary contains only words which, by reason of changes of form or meaning, need to be explained. When the word recurs frequently, every occurrence is not listed, though there is a complete record in each case of orthographic variants.

Proper names, except in a few cases, have not been included, for they are either easily recognizable or discussed in the Notes.

The chief contractions used are the following: *L.*, Latin; *O.E.*, Old English; *O.Fr.*, Old French; *O.H.G.*, Old High German; *O.N.*, Old Norse.

adj., adjective; *adv.*, adverb; *card. num.*, cardinal number; *conj.*, conjunction; *et al.*, et alii; *fig.*, figurative meaning; *NED*, New English Dictionary; *pl.*, plural; *ppl.*, participle; *prep.*, preposition; *pres.*, present tense; *pret.*, preterit tense; *pt. ppl.*, past participle; *s.v.*, sub verbo; *sb.*, substantive; *v.*, verb; *v. sb.*, verbal substantive.

acalden, *v.*, *O.E.* ācealdian; to become cold; **acaldyng** (*pres. ppl.*) 772, 776; **acolde** (*pt. ppl.*) 789.

acordin, *v.*, *O.Fr.*, acorder; agree, accord; **acordiþ, acordeþ** (*pres.*) 68-69, 74, 483; **acordynge, acordyng** (*pres. ppl.*) 70, 99.

acreman, *sb.*, *O.E.* æcer + man; cultivator of the ground, a husbandman, or ploughman; **acremen** (*pl.*) 54, 79.

agaste, *v.*, *O.E.* ā + gæstan; to affright, frighten, terrify, 694.

aȝen-byggynge, *v. sb.*, *O.E.* ongegn + bycgan; redemption, ransom, 1033.

ago, *pt. ppl.*, *O.E.* āgān; gone by, past, 11, 1093.

alleggynge, *v. sb.*, *L.* allēgare; action of adducing as evidence; citing, quoting; the making of an assertion, 245.

an, *prep.*, *O.E.* an, on; on, 669.

anoon, *adv.*, *O.E.* on + ān; straightway, at once, 171, 258, 585, 588.

arst, see *s.v.* **erst.**

araye, *v.*, *O.Fr.* areyer; to prepare oneself, to make ready, 124; **arayed** (*pt. ppl.*) 177; **araying** (*v. sb.*) 68.

asayed, *pt. ppl.*, *O.Fr.* asayer; tried or examined for the sake of information, 366.

assente, *v.*, *O.Fr.* assentir; to agree, give concurrence of one's will to, 388.

assoyle, *v.*, *O.Fr.* assoldre; to acquit oneself of, or to discharge, 148.

auctour, *sb.*, *O.Fr.*, auteur; person who originates or gives existence to anything, who gives rise to a state or condition, 3, 121.

auctorite, *sb.*, *O.Fr.* autorité; power to influence action, opinion, belief, 128, 787, 811.

137

avise, *v.,* *O.Fr.* avīser; to look at mentally, to consider, ponder, 174.

avoutir, *sb.,* *O.Fr.* avoutre; adulterer, 1086.

bayly, baylie, bailie, baylife, baylif, bailif, *sb.,* *O.Fr.* baili; bailiff, administrator, 123, 142, 258, 267, 308, 403; **ballies** *(pl.)* 366.

bailie, baylie, balie, baylye, bayle, balye, bailye, *sb.,* *O.Fr.* baillie; stewardship, administration, 120, 136, 232, 402, 307, 347, 575, 750.

bisse, *sb.,* *O.Fr.* bysse; fine linen, 561.

brasile, *sb.,* *Fr.* bresil; scarlet cloth, 562.

brenne, *v.,* *O.N.* brenna, *O.E.* bernan, bærnan; to burn, 413, 414, 555; **brennynge,** *(v. sb.)* 559; **brent** *(pt. ppl.)* 1077.

but ȝif, *conj.,* *O.E.* būtan gif; unless, except, 32, 33, 34, 36, 63.

bygge, *v.,* *O.E.* bycgan; to buy, 201.

bynemen, *v.,* *O.E.* bi-, beniman; to take away; **bynemeþ** *(pres. pl.)* 396.

bysinesse, *sb.,* *O.E.* bysig + nesse; industry, diligence, 471.

bytaken, *pt. ppl.,* *O.E.* bi + *O.N.* taka; entrusted, committed, 125.

cann, *v.,* *O.E.* cann; to know, know how to; **canst** *(pres.)* 107.

carienes, *sb. pl.,* *O.Fr.* caroigne; carrions, carcases, 672.

certis, *adv.,* *Fr.* certes; certainly, 77, 82, 195 *et al.*

chalenge, *v.,* *O.Fr.* chalengier, calengier; to lay claim to, 522; **challangeþ** *(pres.)* 519.

charge, *sb.,* *O.Fr.* charge, carche; pecuniary burden, expense, 331.

chynche, *sb.,* ? *O.Fr.* chinche; miser, 1086; **chynchis, chynches** *(pl.)* 439, 458.

clepe, *v.,* *O.E.* cleopian, clipian; to summon, bid, invite, invoke, 720, 579; **clepid, clepide** *(pret.)* 11, 17, 139, 98; **clepid, clepeþ, clepliþ** *(pres.)* 15, 20, 25, 602; **clepid, clepud, cleped** *(pt. ppl.)* 98, 367, 403, 590, 168 *et al.;* **clepynge** *(v. sb.)* 175, 209.

cleperis, *sb. pl.,* those who call, 769.

coppe, *sb.,* *O.E.* copp; top or summit of anything, 833.

comite, *sb.,* *O.Fr.* conté; shire court, meeting presided over by the sheriff for transacting legal business of shire, 362.

commeliche, *adj.,* *O.E.* cymlīc; proper, decent, 1067.

contrarien, *v.,* *O.Fr.* contrarier; to do what is contrary to or the reverse of; **contrarie** *(pres.)* 297.

conuersacion, *sb.,* *O.Fr.* conversation; manner of conducting oneself in the world or in society, manner of life, 917.

crafti, *adj.,* *O.E.* cræfti; skillful, 101

cundelich, see *s.v.* **kynde.**

cunnynge, see *s.v.* **kunnynge.**

defaute, *sb.,* *O.Fr.* defaute; absence of something, lack, 49, 55, 65, 286, 363, 625.

deme, *v.,* *O.E.* dēman; to act as judge, to give judgment, 400; **demeþ, demest** (*pres.*) 370, 374, 402; **demynge** (*v. sb.*) 377, 1052.

delicis, *sb. pl.,* *O.Fr.* delice; pleasures, 558.

disalowen, *v.,* *O.Fr.* desalouer; to reject, disown; **disalowid** (*pt. ppl.*) 260.

disparpullid, *pt. ppl.,* *O.Fr.* desparpaillier; dispersed, scattered, 890.

dispendid, *pt. ppl.,* *O.Fr.* despendre; spent, 260.

dispose, *v.,* *O.Fr.* dispōser; to make preparation, prepare oneself, 132.

doctour, doccour, doctourr, *sb.,* *O.Fr.* doctur; teacher, instructor, 277, 3, 288, 375, 488; **doctoures** (*pl.*) 858-859.

duren, *v.,* *O.Fr.* endurer; continue in existence; **durede** (*pret.*) 935.

eken, to ekene, *v.,* *O.E.* ēcan, ȳcan; to increase, add, 339, 641, 651; **eke** (*pres.*) 856.

elengenesse, *sb.,* *O.E.* ælenge + nesse; loneliness, misery, 879.

ellis, *adv.,* *O.E.* elles; otherwise, 55.

endowen, *v.,* *O.Fr.* enduire; to endow; **enduede** (*pret.*) 936.

engyn, *sb.,* *O.Fr.* engin; skill in contriving, cunning, trickery, 514.

ere rowneres, *sb. pl.,* *O.E.* ēare + rūnere; those who whisper in the ears of others, those who spread rumors, 343.

erst, arst, *adv.,* *O.E.* ǣrest; formerly, 415, 243.

eueryb, *sb.,* *O.E.* ǣfre + ǣlc; each one, 84-85; **eueriche, euerych** (*adj.*) every, 122, 258, 224.

eyres, *sb. pl.,* *O.Fr,* heir; heirs, 397.

falshed, *sb.,* *O.E.* fals + hād; falshood, 314.

faute, *sb.,* *Fr.* faute; fault, 363.

fauten, *v.,* *O.Fr.* fauter; to stand in need of, to be deficient in; **fauteþ** (*pres.*) 81.

fayrhed, *sb.,* *O.E.* fæger + hēafod; beauty, 466.

fallen, *v.,* *O.E.* feallan; to fall; **felede** (*pret.*) 950.

felen, *v. pres. pl.,* *O.E.* fēlan; feel, 365.

ferforþ, *adv.,* *O.E.* feorr + forð; far, to a great degree or extent, 697.

fatten, *v.,* *O.E.* fættan; to make fat; **fettid** (*pt. ppl.*) 36.

filþhedis, *sb. pl.,* *O.E.* fȳlð + hād; filtheness, 257.

forbore, *pt. ppl.,* *O.E.* forberan; given up, parted with, 86.

forfeten, *v.,* *O.Fr.* forfaire; to lose by misconduct; **forfeteþ** (*pres.*) 731.

forgoeris, *sb. pl.,* *O.E.* fore + gān; leaders, 908.

forsoþe, *adv.,* *O.E.* for + sōð; truly, 676.

for, *prep.,* *O.E.* for, fær; for, 46, 55, 63 *et al.;* **for** (*conj.*) introducing detailed proof, 27, 29, 33 *et al.;* **for** (*conj.*) so, in order that, 182, 185, 209 *et al.*

forto, *conj.,* *O.E.* for + to; until, 73.

fulfillid, *pt. ppl.,* *O.E.* fulfyllan; filled full, 469, 481, 636;—realized or manifested completely, 655; **fulfillynge** (*v. sb.*) 773, 806.

ȝe, *adv.,* *O.E.* gēa; more than this—marking the addition of something more emphatic, 599.

ȝede, *v. pret.,* *O.E.* ēode; went, 914, 916.

ȝif, *v. pres.,* *O.E.* gifan, giefan; give, 166.

ȝif, *conj.,* *O.E.* gif; if, 32, 38, 50, 53 *et al.* **but ȝif,** see *s.v.* **but ȝif.**

gobet, *sb.,* *Fr.* gobet; a small piece, a lump, 428, 446, 455.

haten, *v.,* *O.E.* hātan; to command; **heet** (*pret.*) 11.

hennes, hennis, *adv.,* *O.E.* heonan; hence, 530, 154.

herde, *sb.,* *O.E.* heorde, hierde; shepherd, 239; **heerdis** (*pl.*) 54.

herfore, *adv.,* *O.E.* hēr + fore; for this reason, 57, 98, 211, 277 *et al.*

hest, *sb.,* *O.E.* hæs; injunction, command, 351; **hestis** (*pl.*) 680.

hiȝe, *v.,* *O.E.* hīgian; to hie, hasten, 359; **hiȝed** (*pt. ppl.*) 691.

hile, *v.,* *O.E.* helian; to protect, cover, 541.

hoo, *adv.,* *O.E.* hwu, hū; how, 290.

houndis, *sb. pl.,* *O.E.* hand, hond; hands, 107.

hynen, *sb. pl.,* *O.E.* hīna?; servants, 817.

into, *conj., prep., O.E.* in + to; until, 510, 907.

jnow, *adv., O.E.* genōh; enough, 63.

knoweleche, *sb.*, from stem of *O.E.* cnāwan; perception or mental ap-
   prehension, 786.
knowlechynge, *sb.*, knowledge, 900.
kynde, *sb., O.E.* cynd; nature, 17, 59, 60, 67, 68 *et al.;* kyndis (*pl.*) 776.
   cyndely, cundelich, *adj.*, 775, 785, 596.
kunne, *v. pres. pl., O.E.* cunnan; know, know how to, 224.
kunnyng, kunnynge, cunnynge, *sb., O.E.* cunnian; knowledge, learning,
   skill, 225, 229, 463.

leeue, *v., O.E.* lēfan, lȳfan; to believe, 921, 864; leeueþ (*pres.*) 741.
lesen, *v., O.E.* lēosan; to lose; leseþ (*pres.*) 450, 451.
leswes, *sb. pl., O.E.* lǣs; pasture lands, 505.
lesynges, *sb. pl., O.E.* lēasung; falsehoods, 1065.
lette, *v., O.E.* lettan; to hinder, desist, 41; lette (*pres.*) 982.
lewid, lewede, *adj., O.E.* lǣwed; lay, not in holy orders, unlearned, 271,
   831.
leyȝede, *v. pret., O.E.* hliehhan; laughed, 394.
liflode, *sb., O.H.G.* lībleita; livelihood, sustenance, 46, 74, 254.
lich, lik, *prep., adj., O.E.* gelīc; like, similar, 283, 5.
liȝe, *sb., O.E.* lēg, līg; flame, 280.
loost, *sb., O.E.* lust; pleasure, desire, 568; lustes, lustis (*pl.*) 798, 280.
lost, *sb., O.H.G.* (far) lust; loss, perdition, 200.
louedrede, *sb., O.E.* luf + rēden; emotion or feeling of love, 158.
louynge, *sb., O.E.* lofung; praise, laudation, 1067.
lowere, *sb., O.E.* hlāford; lord, 342.
lykeþ, *v. pres., O.E.* lōcian; looks, 735.
lymes, *sb. pl., O.E.* lim; *fig.* subjects, 973, 990.

madhede, *sb., O.E.* mād + hād; madness, 729.

mawdementis, *sb. pl., O.Fr.* mandement; commandments, 640.

mayne, meyne, *sb., O.Fr.* maisnee, maisonnée; household, dependents, 1056, 1061.

mede, *sb., O.E.* mēd; reward, meed, 365, 712.

medlid, *pt. ppl., O.Fr.* medler, mesler; mingled, 278.

menis, *sb. pl., O.Fr.* moien; means, 191.

meselrye, *sb., O.Fr.* mesellerie; leprosy, 499.

messageþ, *v. pres. pl., O.Fr.* messager; announce, 768.

mete, *sb., O.E.* mete; food, 70.

meueþ, *v. pres.; O.Fr.* movior, mevoir; suggests, proposes, 843.

middes, myʒttes, *sb., O.E.* in middan; the middle or middle part, 490 606.

moo, *adj., O.E.* mā; more, 535.

Mornynge, Book of, Lamentations of Jeremiah, 212.

morwe, *sb., O.E.* morgen; morning, 6.

mot, *v. pret.-pres., O.E.* mōt; must, with implication of possibility or obligation, 75.

muʒen, *v., O.E.* mugan; to be able; **mowe, mow, mowen, moweþ** *(pres.)* 974, 135, 156, 617, 812, *et al.;* **myʒthen** *(pret.)* 86.

myssayse, *sb., O.Fr.* mesaise; want of ease, 1082; **myeses** *(pl.)* 636.

mynde, *sb., O.E.* mynd; memory, 130.

mys, *adv., O.N.* mis; badly, amiss, 950.

myschef, *sb., O.Fr.* meschef; evil plight, need, 449.

myscheues, *adj.,* unfortunate, distressful, 681.

mysentrid, *pt. ppl., O.E.* mis + *O.Fr.* entrer; entered erroneously, 305.

mysreulid, *pt. ppl., O.E.* mis + *O.Fr.* riuler; badly ruled or governed, 305.

mysuse, *v. pres. pl., O.E.* mis + *O.Fr.* user; use wrongly, 257.

mysvsyng, *sb.,* wrong use or employment, 302.

nede, *adj., O.E.* nēad; necessary, needful, 948; **nede** *(adv.)* necessarily, of necessity, 717.

neþeles, naþeles, *adv., O.E.* ne þe læs; nevertheless, 819, 811.

nis, *v. pres.,* ne + is; is not, 319.

not, noʒt, nouʒt, *pron., adv.; O.E.* nāwiht, nōht; not, nothing, 53, 74, 66, 69, 104, 250, *et al.*

o, oo, on, oon, *adj., card. num.; O.E.* ān; one, 77, 80, 82, 554, 779, 61, 563, 64, *et al.*

or, *prep., O.E.* ǣr; before, 167, 178; see also **oþer.**

ordeynen, *v., O.Fr.* ordener; to set in proper order or condition, to arrange; **ordeynen, ordeyneþ** (*pres.*) **ordeyned** 199, 200, 67, 73; **ordeyned** (*pt. ppl.*) 58, 59, 62.

oþer, or, *conj., O.E.* āhwæðer; or, 102, 106, 108, 101, 165, *et al.*

oþer, *sb., adj., O.E.* ōðer; other one or ones, 140, 151.

oþerwile, *adv., O.E.* ōðer + hwīle; occasionally, 399, 597, 644, 645.

ouþer, oiþer, *conj., O.E.* āhwæðer; either, 239, 240, 511.

ouergoo, *v., O.E.* ofergangan; to spread over so as to cover, 35; **ouergoo** (*pres.*) 964.

oweþ, *v. pres., O.E.* āgan; has, owns, possesses, 509.

owt, out, *sb., O.E.* āwiht; aught, anything, 358, 612, 1022.

owȝtgoynge, *sb., O.E.* ūt + gangan; departure, exit, 739.

paynyme, *sb., O.Fr.* paienisme; a pagan, an infidel, 1048.

peyntoures, *sb. pl., O.Fr.* peint; painters, 284.

pite, *sb., O.Fr.* pité; mercy, repentance, piety, 448, 451, 799.

pleiferen, *sb. pl., O.E.* plega + gefēra; playfellows, companions at play, 336.

plesaunce, *sb., O.Fr.* plaisance; pleasure, 981.

plete, *v. pres., O.Fr.* plaidier; pleads, 357, 361.

poynt—in a poynt, *adv. phr.,* at once, on the instant, 264.

priue, *adj., O.Fr.* privé; intimate, familiar, 810.

Book of Priuytes, Priueytes, Pryueytes, The Revelation of John, 903, 1003, 1047.

proces, processe, *sb., L.* processus; discourse, 122, 137, 516.

queynt, *pt. ppl., O.E.* (ā-)cwencan; extinguished, quenched, 294.

rapeþ, *v. pres. pl., O.Fr.* rape; take by force, 480.

þe raþere, *adv., O.E.* hræðe; all the sooner, all the more quickly, 319, 689.

raueyne, *sb., O.Fr.* ravine; rapine, 408, 416.

rauenes, *adj.,* plundering, 479.

reccheþ, *v. pres. pl., O.E.* rēcan, rēccan; care, consider, 202.

recheles, *adj., O.E.* rēcelēas; negligent, 152.

rede, *v. pres., O.E.* rǣdan; advises, 167, 265, 307, 574, 762, 400.

rekene, *v., O.E.* reccan; to give an account, 259, 404, 580, *et al.*

rekenyng, rekenynge, *sb.,* account, 153, 120, 137, *et al.*

rere, *v., O.E.* rǣran; to lift up, raise, elevate, turn upward, 962; **rere** (*imperative*) 421; **rered** (*pret.*) 431.

reueliþ, *v. pres.,* ? *O.E.* *rifel > rifelede; becomes wrinkled, 727.

reueþ, *v. pres. pl., O.E.* rēafian; rob by force, 256; **reued** (*pt. ppl.*) 412.

rewme, *sb., O.Fr.* realme; realm, 876, 1087.

rygge, *sb., O.E.* hrycg; ridge, back, 338.

ryȝtfulnesse, riȝtfulnesse, *sb., O.E.* riht + fūl; righteousness, 566, 999-1000.

rowneres, see *s.v.* **ere rowneres.**

schameþ, *v. pres., O.E.* sceamian; feels shame in regard to a person, 482.

schrewes, schrewis, *sb. pl., O.E.* scrēawa; wicked or malignant men, 472, 645.

science, *sb., Fr.* science; particular branch of knowledge or study, knowledge, 187.

sclattes, *sb. pl., O.Fr.* esclat; roofing slates, thin slabs of stone, 278.

semblaunt, *sb., Fr.* semblant; a person's outward aspect or appearance, 354.

sentence, *sb., O.Fr.* sentence; judgment, judicial decision, 170.

seyntewarie, *sb., O.Fr.* saintuaire; *fig.* priestly office or order, 215.

siþ, *conj., O.E.* syððan; since, 668, 680, *et al.*

siþþe, *adv.,* next in succession, 256.

skape, *v., O.Fr.* escaper; to escape; 749; **scaped** (*pt. ppl.*) 1100.

soote, *adj., O.E.* swēte; sweet, 547.

soþ, *adj., O.E.* sōð; true, 195, 646; **soþ** (*adv.*) truly, 287. **for soþe,** *adv.,* in truth, truly, 1085.

soþen, *pt. ppl., O.E.* sēoðan; seethed, boiled, cooked, 73.

sore, *adj., O.E.* sār; involving great hardships or painful exertion, 45.

sowneþ, *v. pres., O.Fr.* soner; sounds, is pronounced, 217.

spensis, *sb. pl., O.Fr.* dispense; expenses, 708.

spere, *v., O.E.* sparrian; to shut, exclude, 1061; **spered** (*pt. ppl.*) 1060.

spilt, *pt. ppl.*, *O.E.* spillan; **killed**, 494.

streyt, streyte, *adj.*, *O.Fr.* estreit; strict, rigorous, 125, 133, 139.

suget, soget, *adj.*, *O.Fr.* subgiet; subject, 102, 701.

sugetis, *sb. pl.*, subjects, 236.

sue, swe, *v.*, *O.Fr.* sewir, suir; to follow as an example, or to follow by logic or reasoning, 923, 1012; **sweþ** (*pres.*) 861.

swyche, *adj.*, *O.E.* swylc; such, 251.

swiche, *sb.*, such, 290.

syuyle, *adj.*, *Fr.* civil; civil, 189.

take, *v.*, *O.N.* taka; to give, seize, take, 202; **take** (*pres.*) 320.

tarde venit, *sb.*, *L.*; name of a return made by the sheriff to a writ when it has come into his hands too late to be executed, 365.

teme, *sb.*, *O.Fr.* tesme; theme, instruction, 232.

temperal, *adj.*, *O.Fr.* temporel; concerning interests of the world, secular, 141.

tofore, *prep.*, *O.E.* tōforan; before, in front of, 383, 995.

toʒenes, toʒens, *prep.*, *O.E.* tōgegn, tōgegnes; against, in opposition to, 950, 496-497.

tounne, *sb.*, *O.E.* tunne; tun, cask, 1037.

trowen, *v.*, *O.E.* trēowian; to believe, trust, suppose; **trowe, trowest, trowist** (*pres.*) 711, 398, 414, 259.

trowþe, trewþe, *sb.*, *O.E.* trēowð; faith, truth, 484, 565.

tweye, tweyne, to, two, *card. number*, *O.E.* twēgen; two, 459, 139, 583, 416, 429, 646, *et al.*

þer, *adv.*, *conj.*, *O.E.* þǣr, there, where, 424, 243, 356, 81 *et al.*

þilke, *sb.*, *adj.*, *O.E.* þylc; such, that one, 550, 85, 113, 319, 960, 1015, 1042, *et al.*

vncontinent, *adj.*, *L.* incontinentia; incontinent, 797.

vndirnyme, *v.*, *O.E.* undernyman; to perceive, comprehend, 111, 112.

vnhonest, vnhoneste, *adj., O.E.* un + *O.Fr.* honeste; dishonest, 85-86, 744, 1065.

vnhonestly, *adv.,* dishonestly, disreputably, 274.

vnkunnyng, vnkunnynge, *sb., O.E.* un + cunnian; ignorance, 169, 243.

vnkynde, vnkyndely, vnkendely, *adj., O.E.* uncynde + līc; unnatural, 796, 597, 778, 780, 785.

vnmyȝti, vnmyȝty, *adj., O.E.* unmihtig; weak, powerless, 813, 925.

vnmylde, *adj., O.E.* unmilde; harsh, rough; 797.

vnneþe, *adv., O.E.* unēaðe; scarcely, hardly, with difficulty, 611.

vnobedient, *adj., O.E.* un + *O.Fr.* obeissant; disobedient, 114, 715, 795.

vnpite, impiete, *sb., L.* in + *O.Fr.* pité; impiety, 426, 447, 455.

vnresonable, vnresounable, *adj., O.E.* un + *O.Fr.* raisonable; excessive in amount or degree, 129, 58, 672.

vnriȝtwisnesse, *sb., O.E.* unrihtwīs + nes; unrighteousness, 490-491.

vsen, *v., O.Fr.* user; to carry on, perform, pursue, follow as a custom, 226; **vsid** (*pt. ppl.*) 219.

vttrewarde, *sb., O.E.* ūtor + weard; extreme or ultimate place for guarding, 172.

venge, *v., O.Fr.* venger; to avenge, 556.

vengeaunce, vengeaunce, *sb., O.Fr.* venjance; retributive infliction of injury, 132, 419, 713; **vengeaunces** (*pl.*) 554.

verey, *adj., O.Fr.* vrai; true, 951.

voide, voyde, *adj., O.Fr.* void; unproductive, 29, 40.

waterleche, *sb., O.E.* wæter + lǣce; fresh water blood sucking worm 461.

weneþ, *v. pres. pl., O.E.* wēnan; hope, suppose, 323.

wexe, *v., O.E.* weaxan; to grow, increase, become, 34, 37, 49; **wexe, wexeþ, wexiþ** (*pres.*) 675, 465, 467, 727; **woxe** (*pt. ppl.*) 631.

whiȝt, *sb., O.E.* gewiht; weight, 424.

wile, *sb., O.E.* hwīl; time, while, 636; **whyles** (*pl.*) 807.

wil, *conj.,* while, 471.

wite, wyten, *v., O.E.* witan; to know, take care of, guard, 138, 208, 871, 995, 996, 1027, 1030, 584; **wite, wote, wyte, wost** (*pres.*) 793, 1085, 901, 154, 784, 345; **wisten** (*pret.*) 598.

wiþoute-forþ, *adv., O.E.* wiðūtan + forð; everywhere without or outside, 956.

wole, wolt, wolleþ, *v. pres.*, *O.E.* willan; is willing, wills, 10, 433, 192, 230, 307, 201, 364, *et al.;* **wolde** (*pret.*) 218.

wombe, *sb.*, *O.E.* womb; stomach, 287.

woned, *pt. ppl.*, *O.E.* wunian; accustomed, 929.

wreche, *sb.*, *O.E.* wrǣc; vengeance, punishment, 813.

writis, *sb. pl. O.E.* writ; written commands or precepts issued in courts, 190, 364.